THE LAST CAPITALIST

THE LAST CAPITALIST
A Dream of a New Utopia

Steve Cullen

with linocuts by the author

FREEDOM PRESS
LONDON
1996

First published
by
FREEDOM PRESS
84b Whitechapel High Street
London E1 7QX
in
1996

© Steve Cullen and Freedom Press

ISBN 0 900384 82 4

Typeset by Jayne Clementson
Printed in Great Britain by Aldgate Press, London E1 7RQ

Contents

Preface

There is much millennial speculation in the features pages of newspapers at the moment about what shape the approaching new century will take. Inevitably, given the rebirth of religion and nationalism as horrible antidotes to the equally horrible world of global capitalism, the pundits are forecasting little but doom and gloom, relieved only by a virtual reality world of high-tech wizardry. In short, the future is being informed by dystopian visions.

It is in answer to such dystopian futures that I have written this utopia, *The Last Capitalist*. But utopian (and dystopian) visions are apt to be misunderstood, often wilfully, as when the American right took Orwell's *1984* for their own purposes. So, I should like to say two things about this utopia. Firstly, the subtitle is important. Just as G.K. Chesterton had to stress the subtitle's importance in *The Man Who Was Thursday: A Nightmare*, so too is *The Last Capitalist*'s subtitle important: *A Dream of a New Utopia*. It is a dream, it is not a Wellsian blueprint for a new world. Furthermore, it is my dream, if you don't like it then you are free to imagine your own utopia.

Secondly, good utopian writing should act as a stimulus to thought. A utopia should beg as many questions as it suggests answers. In that sense this booklet is my contribution to an argument that you have to continue, preferably in a good pub drinking well-cared-for beer.

T.E. Lawrence wrote that all men dream, but it is only those who dream in the daytime that are dangerous. Today, it may be that having any sort of dream is unusual, but we need dreams for our future. And what is clear is that we should dream of a better way of living, and a better way of behaving as human beings, then our utopias may become reality.

Steve Cullen
Edinburgh, 2nd January 1995

1.
Blood Feud?

They say that your life is what you make of it. Well, that's true, but only up to a point. Okay, I can create a personal Gramscian hegemony in my head. That's fantasies and wet dreams to you, bud. But life can be hard if you live in the paradise of Atopia, and you wouldn't mind a few weeks or months in the gritty world of Chicago, or down-town LA, sometime in the first quarter of the twentieth century. Yes, life can be hard if you're living in the past. That's another throwaway reference to the twentieth, if you're interested.

If you live in Oxford, you'll have worked out who I am by now. And if you haven't, I'll tell you. The name's Riordan, Anne Riordan. And I'm a private eye, or would be if we had crime, or fixed occupations in Atopia. In any event, I am what I want to be, so I'm a private dick, a peeper, a gum-shoe. Apart from that, well, I help out down the bike repair centre, work in the greenhouses, do the usual computer stuff, and I'm a trained signal operator on the railway, so I do my stints there, at the Reading junction. Oh, and I pass some time at Our University. I'm something of an aficionado of popular culture in the twentieth century, with special reference to crime. Sometimes I wonder if I'm wasting my time studying ancient history, but someone's got to be able to explain the old concepts, like crime and punishment, to today's generation. And, more to the point, that's how I got on to the case of the Last Capitalist.

I was sitting in one of the old Fellows' Gardens enjoying the sun, which, like everything else, is free, when a tall, narrow woman and a short, fat man came through the gateway and stood blinking in the sunlight. They looked lost, so I shouted over. They didn't hear me at first, with the kids making so much noise playing football, but then I caught their attention and they came over. The thin woman stepped elegantly through the mob of kids, but the fat man stopped to bounce the ball off his stomach. Either that or the kids were having a bit of fun.

The thin woman stood in front of me, smiling. I'd like to say that she looked mean, but she didn't.

"What can I do you for, sister?" I said.

"Oh, so we have got the right woman" she answered. The fat man waddled up, brushing mud off his vest. With a stomach like his you'd think he'd wear more than a bag of string over his paunch, but that's his business.

"You *are* Anne Riordan?" the thin woman continued.

"That's me, sister."

"She your sister, Emilia?" the fat man breathed.

Emilia turned and grinned at him. "Perhaps you should stop here for the weekend, Godfrey, and find out a little about Chandler and Hammett from Anne here."

String vest looked puzzled, but he grinned in a happy way. "Chandler and what?"

Emilia ignored him and turned back to me. I was beginning to like this narrow woman. She was the sort of woman I could do business with, except that no one does business in Atopia.

"So you know Raymond and Dashiell then?" I asked.

She smiled and string vest looked even more puzzled, shrugged his shoulders at me, and shouted over to the kids "Any chance of a game?"

The kids burst out laughing, and waved him over. He waddled off and began to run rings around the kids, much to their delight.

"Godfrey's alright. He just doesn't take anything seriously," Emilia said, sitting down next to me.

"Who does?"

"Very few, thank God," Emilia paused and smiled, "whoever he was."

We sat quietly for a few moments watching Godfrey and the kids. That guy could move. 240 pounds, five eight, but fast. I wouldn't want to go up against him in the Windy City with nothing but a string vest between us.

I turned to Emilia. "Well, sister, what can I do for you? You and Godfrey, that is."

She smiled again. A slow, easy smile. Too easy, perhaps. Or was I just stuck in the twentieth century?

She brushed a lock of blonde hair out of her eyes. If she did that too often I'd be getting the hots, and this was no time for that. It didn't pay to get involved with your clients and, anyway, I had to be fixing bike saddles in a few hours.

"We're from the Fed, the Eastern Fed," she drawled.

"Girls and boys from the big EF, eh?" I drawled back.

She looked at me sideways, gave me a long, slow look, the sort of look that said 'You've left a screw behind, sister'.

"Big EF?"

"Yeah," I drawled, "Eastern Fed, the big EF." We had a crackling duet going.

"Right," she smiled, "the big EF. Yes, me and Godfrey have been sent by the," she paused, "big EF. They thought that you'd be able to help. Or, rather, a woman called Katriana Jayawardena thought you might be able to help, and the Fed's monthly meeting voted to send us down to see you."

"Yeah, I know her. She's involved in the Norfolk History Group. Met her a few times. We share interests."

"That's her. She said that you might be able to help."

"About what?" I shook out a couple of cheroots, but Emilia shook her head at them, so I lit one myself and leant back, watching her through the blue smoke. Only the wind in the quad kept blowing it away.

"About a problem that we might have in the Eastern Federation," she paused, flicked the loose lock of hair again, and looked over to where Godfrey had just been tackled by a little girl with green hair.

"You might have?" I croaked. I'll never get used to the tobacco I grow in my window-ledge.

"Yes, might have. It's the Angries."

"The Angries? You've got some problems with the Angries?" I couldn't keep the surprise out of my voice. There were little groups of Angries here and there. We had some in Oxford. Old-time revolutionaries who hadn't got over the fact that Atopia just evolved, just became, as people forged new ways of doing things. The Angries had wanted a revolution overnight, a big bust-up, a big crack-up with the old-time bosses. But that hadn't happened, so the Angries were still waiting for 'The Day' as they called it. We had Angries here. There was a group of them that lived in what had been All Souls. In fact they were the only full-time residents in the old university buildings. A harmless bunch, spent their time reading, arguing with each other, splitting into factions, re-forming, waiting for 'The Day'. It had arrived, but we didn't tell them that, and no-one cared that they didn't produce anything. They needed to eat like anyone, even if they were weird. They took what they needed from the communal market, just like everyone else. But trouble with the Angries, that was something new.

Emilia looked at me, her blue eyes looked concerned. "Well, we think that we might have. For a start they've actually started talking to people other than themselves, in Lincoln, in Norwich. They're saying that 'The Day' is coming. There's rumours of someone having a gun." Emilia stopped to let that one sink in. Someone with a gun. A gun. When had Atopia last seen someone carry a gun? Not since the old-time army disbanded itself.

I blew tobacco smoke out through my nose, tried not to cough, and leant close to Emilia. I could smell gardenia, or perhaps it was vinegar. I clenched my teeth and spoke. "You'd better tell me the whole story, sister."

She looked puzzled. "What?"

I unclenched my teeth, let the coughing fit out and threw my cheroot away. When I'd finished coughing I said again "Tell me the whole story."

Emilia leant back on the bench, drew a deep breath and started. "I don't know how much you know about the Eastern Federation, but we're organised on similar lines to the Ox and Bucks Federation, only given that we've more smallholders, our organisation tends to be much looser. Things take time. You know how things are." I grunted. I'd have to give up growing tobacco. "Anyway," she continued, "sometime early last year a rumour started that there was a capitalist in Lincolnshire."

"A what?" This story was getting crazier by the minute.

Emilia nodded. "I know. I know it's hard to believe and, to tell the truth, the Fed's not sure that it's much more than a rumour. Even the delegates from the area couldn't give us concrete information."

"Which area is that?" I was getting interested now, and I'd taken my notebook out.

"That's the funny thing. The capitalist was supposed to have first been heard of in Grantham."

That was really weird. Grantham was the historical heart of Atopia. The first People's Council had been formed there, by-passing the old, unrepresentative council. And from the Grantham's People's Council and then the Lincolnshire Alliance the whole idea had spread. A capitalist in Grantham. It was grotesque.

"Yes, Grantham." Emilia paused, fiddling with the loose lock of hair, "The first reports were that someone had tried to barter goods that had come from outside the Eastern Fed, but with the intention of taking a percentage for doing nothing. Then the rumour was that graffiti had appeared on walls saying 'Profit Makes One Free' and 'All Power to Profit', 'Entrepreneurship. Now!'. All fairly obscure stuff that no-one took any notice of. Even if it did exist, and we haven't established that yet."

Godfrey was showing the kids how to do a scissors kick. He obviously had a knack with the kids. That's the way it is, you learn what you need to learn. It's all there, and there's plenty of Godfreys to show the kids how. I dragged my eyes away from Godfrey's stomach, and back to the case. "But what have the Angries got to do with this, this capitalist, if he or she exists" I said.

"I was coming to that. There aren't any Angries in Grantham, but when the Lincoln Angries got wind of it – they're living in the old cathedral – they took it as a sign. They called in all the outlying Angries for a special Trotsky-Bukharin congress, and their leaders decided that the Grantham capitalist meant that the final conflict is on the way, and their time has come. To put it bluntly, we think that they're hoping for a violent revolution."

"But against who?" I asked.

"The capitalist."

"One? Just one capitalist, who mightn't exist anyway?"

"The Angries claim that it shows that Atopia is a bourgeois state."

"A state?" I almost asked what that was, but as I said, I'm well-versed in ancient history.

We both sat in silence for a while. The kids had wandered off, leaving the ball on the grass. Godfrey was lying on his back, steam rising through the holes in his vest.

"Well, how can I help?" I asked.

"At the big monthly meeting, after voting in new delegates, the Fed decided that we must look into this, that we had to find out if this capitalist really exists. We need to find this capitalist, if he or she is out there, so that we can find out what the problem really is."

"But you don't know how to go about it, is that it?"

Emilia nodded. "You know some history, when did anyone in Atopia need to investigate anyone else. Shit, that's policing, that's for governments."

"You're right there, sister."

"So then Katriana suggested that you might know how to go about it. You know, tracking someone, finding them."

It sounded like a case to me. My first case. But I had a conscience, after all, I was an anarchist.

"But there's a problem, sister, I'm just a theorist in that department. If you want me to fix a bike, grow melons, propagate fruit trees, do a bit of printing, programme a computer, help you give birth, fine, I'm your woman. But find a capitalist, find someone who doesn't want to be found. I don't know. Perhaps I can't help."

Emilia turned her big blue eyes on me. "You've only got the theory, but Anne, we haven't even got that."

I was doubtful, and I must have looked it.

"Anne, you've got to, for the people's peace of mind, for Atopia. Anne, there's something else."

I looked at her. "What's that?"

"The Angries are talking of a blood feud, a blood feud that they have to fight against the capitalist, or capitalists as they are now saying. Blood! Fighting, killing, we don't need that, there's no place for it in Atopia. Anne, you know your history, that all went in the old times, that's why Atopia grew. It was how Atopia won, without hate, without violence. We don't need it."

A shadow fell on us both. It was Godfrey, his bulk blotting out the sun. "She's right, Anne. If blood is ever spilt again, who knows what might happen. You've got to help."

I'd liked to have said 'Fifty dollars a day, plus expenses, and a two hundred dollar retainer', but that would have been plain daft. I'd just swap my work on this for something from the Eastern Fed, so I nodded and said, "I'm your woman. You can go and tell the Fed that."

Godfrey shook my hand and Emilia kissed me. I was glad it wasn't the other way round.

*   *   *

I saw Emilia and Godfrey off from the station, and took the opportunity to see the Oxford-Reading train co-ordinator, Nathanial Smoke, to ask if he thought the local rail committee would be able to spare me for a fortnight. When I explained what it was about, he said he couldn't see why not. Smoke is a decent bloke. Completely gone about the railway, one of the few full-timers on it, in fact, but a good bloke. I've known him for years, right back to when he called himself Fossdyke Gooch, but since then he's changed his name a few times, and now he's Smoke.

I called in at 'The Navvy's Honour' and picked up eight bottles of their best ale. I'd helped brew it, so I knew it was good. I'd need a few drinks to help me think my way through this case.

*   *   *

My home is an old boat on the canal, 'Berkman's Barge' some wit had called it in the past. It had been allocated to me by the Water Dwellers and Bargees Association, no charge, all I had to do was maintain it in good order, and I could call on them for any major help I needed with 'Berkman'. Anyway, it suited me fine. I suppose I'm not as communal as some people think I should be, like the people out in Malatesta Towers. But that's fine, they don't bother me and I don't bother them.

'Berkman's Barge' wallowed in the clear water, and moved under me as I leapt aboard. A blackbird was busy announcing the arrival of spring from the pollards that ran up from the canal bank. Smoke drifted up from the barge next to 'Berkman', the palest grey in the evening light. The buckets of daffodils that I had on the deck were intensely yellow. I stood admiring them for a while, and then went down below with my ale.

It was warm below and with a few glasses of ale inside me I began to drift away from the problem of the last capitalist. Or was he or she really the first capitalist? Wood shifted in my little stove, I drank some more and closed my eyes. Trotsky came forward to greet me. He was wearing the insignia of a Red Army general. Someone else was being prepared for a firing squad. I tried to look to see who it was, but Trotsky's head got in the way. There was something sticking out of it. A nineteenth century capitalist, in top hat and tails, floated by like a balloon. Then Emilia swam into view, she was messing with her hair, and she was wearing nothing but Godfrey's string vest. I noticed that it was too big for her. I had to go to Grantham, but I couldn't find the place, it was hidden by all the black flags. 'Berkman's Barge' shifted, and I knocked the back of my hand against my glass. I jumped suddenly, like you do in a dream, the glass went over and I opened my eyes. Someone was coming down the ladder into the cabin. He wore heavy boots and a long brown coat, cut in seventeenth century style with deep turned-back cuffs edged with yellow. One hand was held out. The hand was very white, and it gripped a gun.

2.
The Road to Grantham

What gave John Clare away was ignorance, as usual. He was holding the gun by the barrel, pointing it at himself, in fact.

"Come along in, John," I said, "I've a couple of pints of the Navvy's best here, but I expect you knew that already."

John eased his big body into the cabin and stood there, his head touching the ceiling. He waved the butt of the gun at me. "How about that, then. Didn't think I could get one for you, did you? Admit it, you didn't think I'd find one of these gun things."

I smiled. John was one of those blokes you went to when you wanted something unusual, or antique, like a car or, in this case, a gun for the museum of twentieth century culture that a group of us were trying to set up in the city library.

I pushed a glass towards John, and began to pour out the ale. "Sit down, have a drink, and tell me how you found it."

John stuck his big-booted feet under the table, pushed the gun towards me and lifted his glass. "Wassail!"

"Wassail, John."

"Found it in London. It doesn't work, like. At least, I don't think it works. But it'll do for the museum, eh?"

I fingered the rusty revolver. It was strange to think that in the old days so much had depended on guns and other weapons. No wonder the world was crazy back then, no wonder people had finally got sick to death of killing, and getting ready to kill, and turned their backs on the whole damn thing. That had been one of the first great steps. The old time peace movements were honourable antecedents of Atopia.

"Yes, it'll be great for the museum. What do we owe you for it?"

"Well," John paused to take another mouthful of Navvy's best, "it cost me three days working on building a house for a self-build group, and looking after a couple of little kids for a weekend."

"That was a lot."

"It's a rare item. Very rare. To tell the truth, Anne, I'd never seen one of those things until that one."

"That makes two of us. So, what do you want for it?"

He leant back in his chair, his long, brown coat dragging on the floor, his big face calm, pleasant, content.

"How about the equivalent of two days hoeing on my smallholding by a couple of you museum types, and some help from you with my computer?"

"Done!"

I poured out the dregs of the beer into our two glasses, and we drank to the agreement.

John put his empty glass down and looked at it sadly. "Fancy making an evening of it with a few in the 'Gardener's Arms'?"

I shook my head. "I'd like to, John, but I'm getting ready for a trip to Lincolnshire, to Grantham in fact."

"Grantham? More history work, eh?"

"In a way. I'm looking for a capitalist."

John's face opened and he let out his great booming laugh. When he'd finished he said, "That's a good one. That makes looking for a gun sound easy."

* * *

There were a couple of kids that I'd not seen before painting the front of the waiting room on platform two. I went over to have a chat with them. The youngest, a tall, thin lad of about twelve who called himself Long Tom, put his brush down and sat on my bag to tell me about a butterfly project that he was involved in. It was part of the project to try and fix up some of the damage that had been done in the centuries before the triumph of the utopians. He was responsible for a colony of chalk-hill blues, whatever they were. Tom certainly knew his stuff, and the lists of Latin names of butterflies, moths and their associated plants left me standing. He had that open, secure, happy way most kids have. He asked me what I was interested in, what work I did. I told him, and he said that he was doing some basic computer work so perhaps we'd meet up again. I said I hoped so, and waved goodbye to the two painters as the long, black engine pulled in with its train.

It was an early train so the carriage was fairly empty. I sat back and looked out of the window, waiting for the glimpses of Oxford through the woodland that surrounded the city and provide most of our timber needs. The engine began to pick up speed after Banbury, and

I sank back, thinking about the case and the journey.

I wasn't at all sure how to go about finding the last capitalist. Things were going to be difficult. This was Atopia, not the USA at the beginning of the twentieth century. People knew the score then, they were familiar with crime, detectives, police, DAs, lying, all the baggage of old world life. But how would I get on now? I'd have no trouble getting information, people invariably gave you straight answers, there was no reason to hide anything, but would they take it as a great joke? Detective? A capitalist? 'Who are you kidding, that's a good one ...' I could hear it now. I was going to have my work cut out.

The train slowed, and stopped at a small wayside halt. An old woman, well into her seventies, wandered along the platform shouting out the details of the train. A little white dog followed at the hems of her black trousers. They were both taking it easy. But then it was useful work, not useless toil. Doors slammed, the old woman blew her whistle, the dog barked and the train pulled out, past a young woman and two little children who stood and waved at the departing train.

The railways were one of the prides of Atopia. Historically they were one of the great examples that helped build Atopia, and now they were a living example of voluntarism and co-operation on a national scale. Under the old system the railways had been reduced to a few main lines, dominated by an oligarchy of travel companies. Most of the country was left without railways at all. But that only served as a spur to the local networks of enthusiasts' lines. There were plenty of these groups in existence anyway, such as the Didcot group that was the origin of the Oxford-Reading line that I work for. But the new circumstances meant that the combination of nostalgia, enthusiasm and the local demand for transport for all brought dozens, then hundreds, of local lines into existence. At first they were unconnected to each other, but under pressure from the big oligopolists who feared for their profits, the little lines formed into a National Railway Federation. At first the NRF was formed merely as an information and pressure group network, but then they saw the rationale of linking up their lines where they could. As most of the little railways were run by volunteers and enthusiasts, their costs were much lower than the oligopolists. They served local communities who backed them up in the fight they had to face with the oligopolists and the rail unions, who still stuck to old concepts of employed labour. But the great decline in paid full-time employment meant that the voluntarists had history on their side. Then the oil really did run out, and by then the voluntary, co-operative, work not toil, ethos held sway and the NRF lines provided the backbone of long distance, and local, travel throughout the new Atopia.

We were on time when we reached Nottingham, where I had to change for the train to Grantham. The local trains are always the busiest, and the most eccentric. Not in terms of punctuality, which, by all accounts, is as good as it had always been, but in terms of liveries and rolling stock. The Brighton-London line's the best I've been on, with potted plants, samovars and a library on each train, in addition to all the high-tech stuff you expect.

The train to Grantham left bang on time, driven by a bearded septugenarian with a young girl with only one arm sitting next to him in the cab, learning the trade. The Notts-Grantham people must have adapted cabs for people like her.

I was only going so far as Bottesford on this train, then I'd get off and walk the last seven miles or so into Grantham. I prefer to arrive on foot in any town that's new to me. And anyway, I felt that I should make a little attempt at a pilgrimage to Grantham, the home of anarchy, the famous 'Black Banner Town'.

I'd sat opposite a couple with two little kids. I did the decent thing and asked how old they were.

The bigger one spoke first. "I'm six, and Amy's ..."

The smaller one piped up, "I'm not Amy, not anymore. I'm Robert. And I'm five."

The couple laughed. "She's four," the bloke said, "and she's always changing her name. She'll fix on a few steady choices soon enough, just like the rest of us."

I smiled at Robert, and she smiled back. "I've got a friend who's an astronomer," she started. That's the only problem about travelling on the train, you keep meeting kids who know far more about far more subjects than you know yourself. If you want to find out about the cutting edge of science or arts, just ask a kid, he or she will bound to know someone who's a surgeon, an agriculturalist, a midwife or an astronomer.

"They've found Planet X, you know."
I didn't, but I listened and found out, all the way to Bottesford.

*   *   *

The train hummed away down the line, I shouldered my bag, pulled my hat down and left the station with its bright paintwork, and banks of daffodils, narcissi and patches of aconite under the poplars around the bike park. I headed out of Bottesford on the Grantham road.

There were a few bicyclists riding in and out of Bottesford, but after a mile or so I had the road to myself. The sun was still quite low in the sky, despite the warmth of an early spring, so I walked in the middle of the road. It was strange to think that in the past walking in the middle of this road, any road, would have been a suicidal act. It was difficult to imagine the noise, the pollution and the sheer strangle-hold on life that the old internal combustion engine had in the past. In the medieval period families shared their homes with their animals but, absurdly, in the age of the car they'd shared their lives and homes with cars! At least cow shit was useful, unlike car fumes. How old fashioned, so totally out of date, the age of the car seems. Thank god the oil did run out. Not that the car had much of a future even before then. The massive road-building programme, along with new methods of car production, meant that there were just too many cars on the road. People spent far too much time and effort paying for their cars, paying car taxes, paying to use roads, insuring their cars, protecting them, sitting in them going nowhere except to the next gridlock. Like everything else in the old world, they realised they had to find new ways of living. And abandoning the car meant developing different ways of working, which led to a different attitude to life, which all pushed us on the road to Atopia.

I kept walking on the warm, quiet road that cut through the flat fields surrounded by thick hedges and intensively worked copses, through the countryside busy with human as well as animal life. I was getting hungry, but I couldn't see any pub near, so I took my bag off and lay in the grass by the road to have the bottle of beer and the few sandwiches I'd brought along. Tiny blue and white flowers, like stars, nestled in the grass, and as I was peering at one of them I heard footsteps on the road. A man dressed in a long grey cloak and carrying a walking stick came up.

"Hi there," he smiled, "any chance of a beer?" He nodded to the bottle that I'd opened.

"Sure, sit down."

I rummaged in my bag and pulled out another bottle. He reached out and took it.

"Thanks." He squinted at the label on the bottle, "Hey! Oxford Ale, brewed at the 'Eagle and Child'. That's good ale, man! Oxford Ale!"

He was pleased. I was pleased. Oxford beers were famous. We clinked bottles. "Wassail!"

"Wassail!"

"The name's Jack, Jack-by-the-Hedge. And yours?"

"Anne Riorden, from Oxford."

"And going to the Black Banner Town?"

"That's right."

"A pilgrimage?"

I smiled. Perhaps I shouldn't shout it around about my true mission. Perhaps the capitalist was working his old-style magic on me, making me as distrustful as people were in the old days.

"Yes, I'm on a sort of pilgrimage."

Jack looked up at the blue sky with its great billowing clouds. "Great day for it. Great days we have."

I looked at the happy man with his brown face, his cloak and his stick, with the bundle of waterproof on his back.

"You a Wanderer?" I asked.

"Yeah, that's right. The only life for me. Just walk the roads, meet the people, work when you want, eat where you will, sleep where you will. Yes, I'm a wanderer on the roads. But I spend the winters indoors. I like to write and print my magazine, something to pass out to folks as I go on the road in the spring, summer and fall."

He began to root around in his waterproof sack. Eventually he found what he was looking for, a bundle of small digest-sized magazines.

"Hey, perhaps you've heard of it, my pride and joy."

"I don't know, what's your magazine called?"

"Here," he passed me a copy, "it's called *Gandalf's Garden*."

I took the small, thick magazine, turning it over in my hands. There was a good illustration on the front cover. "Woodcut?" I asked, nodding at the cover.

"Yeah, do you like it?"

"It's good."

"Thanks. All my own work."

I wasn't sure if he wanted me to start reading it, so I opened it and looked at the title page, which was headed by Landauer's famous maxim, 'The state is not something which can be destroyed by a revolution, but is a condition, a certain relationship between human beings, a mode of human behaviour; we destroy it by contracting other relationships, by behaving differently'. I looked back at Jack-by-the-Hedge. "You're in the tradition, then?"

"Sure. But I like to think of myself as being a bit, you know, of a mystic. A bit from the east, a bit from England – 'One of the Lords of No Man's Land, good Lob' – a bit from the old days even, sort of a successor to the New Travellers."

"You mean the people the old world tried to stamp out, legislate out of existence?" I asked.

"Yeah, that's them. Funny, in the past I'd be illegal, what they used to call a criminal. Imagine, old Jack being a crime," he laughed, throwing his head back, laughing at the clear light sky.

We finished up the beer and my sandwiches and headed off down the road again.

"I'll be leaving you soon, I said I'd help a bloke fix his roof over there," he swung his arm in the direction of a thick plantation of Scots pines.

We walked in a friendly silence. I liked this man in the grey cloak, tapping his way down the bright road with a stack of *Gandalf's Gardens* in his pack. Open and friendly. Who the hell could be afraid of him. Yet he was the bogey-man of yesterday.

We reached a fork in the road and Jack turned to me. "I'm going this way. Thanks for the beer. Brewed at the 'Eagle and Child' eh! The beer for me," he grinned, "I'd like to meet you again, Anne."

"Perhaps we will."

He walked off, I blew him a kiss, and he climbed over a gate into a ploughed field. I turned back to the road. For a while I could hear his voice singing out that famous song, 'This Land Is Your Land'. Like he said, he was a bit of every tradition.

3.
In the Black Banner Town

These are the flat lands, but I was pretty close to Grantham before I saw the first of its famous black banners. The town is ringed by them, a forest of black cloth waving in the wind that finds its way across the North Sea, quickly scours the Wash and hurries to blow life into the black flags of Grantham. The first town to declare itself free from government, free from compulsion and coercion. The first town to unanimously declare for co-operation, non-violence and voluntary association. Grantham – the Black Banner Town.

But was there something nasty in the heart of Atopia? Was there really a capitalist in Grantham? And was he or she the last or the first capitalist we had? Walking between the long avenue of black banners into the town, I found it hard to believe that there could be any association between Grantham and capitalism. It seemed to be so absurd, unbelievable. And the idea of asking people about a capitalist in the midst of their black flags seemed laughable.

*   *   *

A cyclist was riding slowly towards me, letting her bike meander across the road in an aimless, relaxed manner. She smiled as she came closer to me. "Hi there! You a pilgrim?" She stopped and got off her bike, wheeling it towards me. She was a small, dark woman with long, neatly plaited, black hair.

"In a way," I answered. I hadn't yet decided how to approach people over the capitalist. Some private eye I was turning out to be, couldn't even ask the right questions.

"In what way?" she asked, looking at me with big, open eyes.

"Actually," I hesitated, "I'm here on behalf of the Eastern Fed. I'm here about the capitalist business."

She laughed, a clear, light laugh that made you think of clear streams and the sun. "Oh that! Our famous capitalist. He's gone, or she's gone. Anyway, it's gone. That's the word."

"Gone. Yes, I think I knew that."

She looked at me with pity.

"That's not as silly as it sounds," I said, "I still need to find out what I can about your famous capitalist."

She laughed again. "I can't see why." She started to get back on her bike, "But if you're really interested you want to visit 'The Woolpack', the landlord there claims that he's met the capitalist."

She began to cycle off, shouting over her shoulder, "But I'd say that he's been drinking too much of his own beer."

"Thanks. I'll go and see. Beer and landlord that is" I shouted after the meandering cyclist.

I watched her wander away, taking her happy, free laughter with her.

She hadn't told me where to find 'The Woolpack', but I shouldn't have any problems there. Pubs were really at the centre of communal life in Atopia. They were the great centres of cultural and social activity for all people, not just the beer drinkers. Without our pubs we'd be nothing, there'd be no utopia. But it hadn't always been like that. In the past, before the great popular movement to a better way of living, the pubs had been in the grip of a small clique of brewers. That in itself was hard to imagine, pubs not selling their own ale brewed on site but relying on huge breweries. The horror of it! But it was worse, as from the end of the twentieth century the big brewers had begun to squeeze their tenants, forcing them out with higher and higher rent increases and closing down pubs all across Britain. That had been another of the changes that helped the growth of autonomous life. Just as the activities of the railway oligopolists had led to more independent action, so did the great closure of pubs lead to the start of the independent inns movement, backed by one of the few really successful, ground-up, protest movements of the old regime – CAMRA. Those good people, like the rebels of the Anti-Poll Tax Movement of the late twentieth century, were real heroes.

*   *   *.

I walked slowly into Grantham, singing snatches of 'He's the man, the very fat man, who waters the workers' beer ...' and keeping my eye out for 'The Woolpack'. I was getting thirsty, it was getting late and I could do with a bed.

I needed directions, so I crossed the road to ask a group building

new houses. I ducked under a sign announcing that the houses on this plot were being built by the 'Colin Ward Self-Build Association', and stepped through piles of builders' rubble to speak to a young lad shovelling wet concrete out of an electric mixer into a wheelbarrow. He looked up as I slipped on some broken tiles.

"Hi. Mind those tiles," he grinned, and shovelled more concrete.

"Good job you warned me," I said, "I might have slipped otherwise."

He laughed and stopped shovelling. "An ironist, eh?"

"No, I'm a computer programmer and greenhouse ace, if you must know."

He groaned and stepped forward to shake my hand. I let him rub a fistful of concrete into my palm, then said, "Could you help me, I'm looking for 'The Woolpack'. Which way is it?"

He didn't answer my question, but said "I thought you weren't from around here."

"Neither are you for that matter," I replied.

"Right, I'm up from the smoke. Fancied working out in a country town for a while. And," he nodded to the unfinished houses, "I like building, makes me feel good. In small doses that is. I'll be moving on when we've finished these last two. Wouldn't mind doing some telecom work for a while. I'm trained on hotwave transmitters."

He was obviously going to talk for a while. What the hell. I wasn't in a hurry, and I liked looking at him. Nice brown eyes, and his jeans fitted.

"We've made some good houses here," he continued, "all the latest technology. Won't be a drain on any resource practically. One of the finest green-build homes you'll find in the Black Banner. And they're a good bunch to work with, the Ward bunch. Yes," he scratched his short cropped hair, letting the blue stubble spring under his concreted fingers, "yes, I've enjoyed working here."

I marvelled that a kid like this could talk so much.

"And they've been generous too, given me a bonus of ten Work Scrip a week, on top of the Scrip for the work I've done. And they've got some bloody good craftsmen and women here. There's a bloke called Jacques Le Goff, Welsh bloke, who can do anything, and I mean anything, with a lump of stone. Finest stonemason I've ever come across."

The concrete lad hesitated and I took my chance. "Yes, it sounds great. But could you tell me how I can find 'The Woolpack'? I could do with a pint and a bite to eat."

"'The Woolpack'? Yeah, no problem, just across the road, round the corner. Nice place. I've been staying there. Great beer, nice little wood out the back too, kids like playing there. I'll see you there later on, I always have a few before I turn in," he grinned at me, almost a leer I thought. Still, he did fit those jeans.

"Thanks" I said, slipping over the broken tiles again and beating a retreat towards 'The Woolpack'.

"Mind those tiles" he called, then turned back to the concrete.

I ducked under the Colin Ward sign and picked my way back onto the road. Self-build. I often wondered how we ever built our homes other than by self-build. How else could you do it? How else could you get the house that you needed, that fitted your individual requirements, your needs, your desires? And how else could you create a community from the outset? Self-build groups, like everyone else, made use of extra workers like the lad I'd been talking to, but all self-build groups had one thing in common: if you wanted to live in the group's houses you had to work on them. I laughed out loud. How the hell did we ever build homes before? Neither bureaucrats nor profiteers, but self-build.

*   *   *

'The Woolpack' stood back from the road, fronted by a garden full of spring bulbs. Fruit trees were espaliered across the front of the pub and along a red-bricked wall that ran out from the left hand side of the building. Over the wall I could see a mixture of trees, each covered in hints of green. A cat lay curled among some daffodils by the door. I bent and stroked it before opening the door and going in.

There was a baby asleep in a basket on the bar. It was breathing gently, sleeping peacefully unaware of the voices and laughter from the dozen or so people in the large room hung with pictures of old Lincolnshire and various heroes of the past – General Ludd, Captain Swing, Bakunin, Wat Tyler, Bart De Ligt, Proudhon, William Cobbett, Fred Woodworth and even a rather proletarian looking Robin Hood. That seemed doubtful to me, but, so what?

A barrel-chested bloke sporting a huge grey beard stood behind the bar beneath an enormous picture of Kropotkin. Greybeard unfolded his thick arms and stepped towards his taps, smiling and saying "And what can I fix you, friend?"

I dropped my bag and stepped up to the bar. "A pint of your best, landlord." That was straight out of a Victorian gaslight scene, but barrel-chest didn't seem to mind. He reached down a pewter pot and pulled the pint, the enamelled handle looking tiny in his great grasp. "I'm also looking for a bed for the night, can you help me there?" I asked.

He smiled again. "Sure, plenty of beds this time of year, the Wanderers aren't all out on the roads yet. Soon have you sleeping as happily as Errico there," he nodded towards the sleeping baby.

"Yours?" I asked.

He didn't speak but just let his smile grow until it split his beard in half. Yes, the softly sleeping Errico was his.

The landlord came round the bar and picked up my bag. "I'll take your bag upstairs. You hungry?"

"I am."

"What would you like, game pie, vegetarian haggis or beef butties?"

"The beef butties will do fine," I replied.

He stepped over to a small white door, opened it, filled the space it revealed, then turned back to me. "Will you be giving us a hand while you're here, or ...?"

"If I can. If you've a greenhouse or need a bit of high-tech help, computers, bikes ..."

"A chat about computers would be okay."

"Right then," I smiled at him.

Greybeard nodded and disappeared behind the white door. I drank my beer, watched Errico, waited for my beef butties and mine host who, I hoped, would be able to give me my first real lead in the case.

Ten minutes later he reappeared, a huge pile of beef butties, onions, celery and cheese in his hand. I took the food from him with thanks. He looked at me more closely now. "You're not a Wanderer, are you?" he asked.

"No I'm not." I still hadn't decided how to approach asking people about the capitalist, and I didn't want to open by telling Greybeard that I was a detective, assuming he knew what that was.

The name's Anne Riordan, and yours?"

"Maximillian Arbuthnot," he grinned, "for the moment."

"Fine beer you brew, Maximillian."

"Call me Max."

"Fine beer, Max."

"It should be," he grinned with pride, a grin nearly as big as the one he'd given on behalf of the sleeping Errico, "only the best ingredients. I travel to Kent myself to choose the hopes, and I can tell you I know my hops."

"I can taste that."

I took another bite at a beef buttie and looked at Max. I felt that I needed to talk a little more before I broached the topic of the capitalist. Damn, it would have been a lot simpler in Marlowe's day – that's Philip, not Kit – I'd have just had to wave a folded bill under Max's nose and he'd have given me the goods. Well, he'd have told me a pack of lies, but I'd have been able to see through them. It was a pity people had lost the lying habit, it must have made everything so simple in the old time, you simply distrusted everyone. You knew where you were. But Max. Who could distrust him, the great baby-minder and beer brewer.

"How do you manage the exchange with the Kentish growers?" I asked.

That was cunning, it would be a lead in to the capitalist. I was slipping into my twentieth century persona.

"Eastern Fed Work Scrip. They're quite happy with that down there. They don't produce much of their own scrip in Kent, but they'll use ours, it's good throughout Atopia. We also do some direct exchanges too," he laughed, and I mean laughed. When the Woolpack had stopped shaking he carried on. "Sort of coals to Newcastle. I swap them on the basis of my apples. Apples to Kent, good, eh? But," he leaned closer to me across the bar, "I've got the help of a great husbandman here, she's the finest worker with apples that I've ever seen. She could graft an apple tree onto a nettle. And a pretty mean lathe-turner she is too."

I nodded. "Apples and Work Scrip. Eastern Fed Scrip, I've seen that a few times in Oxford. We produce our own local Work Scrip there. How long is your Scrip valid?"

"Currently six months, but a few years ago the Fed delegates voted for a trial of a year and there's talk of something between the two, perhaps nine months. The Woolpack's a verifying agency, just like all the pubs and post offices in Grantham."

*   *   *

A crowd suddenly burst into the bar calling for beer and food. Max excused himself and began serving the ale, while two of the newcomers went behind the bar to the kitchen to fix the food. I was left with the still sleeping Errico, my butties and the beer. I started thinking about the Work Scrip system, one of the ways that the economies of Atopia kept going and the main way we rewarded work that was done entirely in the private domain, such as housework. The Work Scrip system was another pre-utopian idea that had helped to build the alternative world that led to the emergence of Atopia. The system had grown out of the semi-formalising of the black economy, as it was strangely called, in the 1980s when local groups of people developed increasingly sophisticated ways of avoiding the government's taxes. Forming loose groups of workers, people could either swap one service directly for another – you paint my house, I'll fix your car, that sort of thing – or issue credit notes for work done that could be exchanged with different people in the group. A little later than this spontaneous development, renewed interest was shown in the theories of Silvio Gesell who'd put forward an idea of stamp-scrip money that fulfilled the function of a medium of exchange but wasn't a store of value, thereby preventing the accumulation of capital and the lending of money on the basis of interest charging. Gesell's idea was later adapted to the changed demands of the newly-established Atopia. Instead of having to purchase stamps from the government to keep your stamp-scrip in date, each note of work done, the Work Scrip, only had a life of so many months, after that it was worthless. So you had to spend your 'money' which had no intrinsic value in itself but was merely a note of work done and could be used as a means of exchange. When you handed your Work Scrip to someone else they took it to a verifying centre where they had their initials and the new start date stamped on it.

*   *   *

Errico woke up, stared at me in the surprised sudden way that waking babies stare at anything, then laughed. I smiled at him, but he didn't like that and closed his eyes again. Max came over and looked into the basket. "Are you awake again Errico, my little mate?"

The baby opened his eyes at the sound of Max's voice, wiggled, waved his hands and began to laugh a low, chuckling laugh. Max lifted Errico out of his basket and presented him to me. "He's a cheerful little fellow, always smiling."

I cradled the smiling Errico in my arms and grinned back at Max. We must have looked pretty daft, three grinning idiots.

"Another beer?" asked Max pointing to my empty glass.

"Please."

Errico snuggled against me until Max returned from the pump with my beer. We swapped baby and beer and I toasted Errico, "Wassail, little fellow!"

Errico seemed pleased.

"Max, I was just thinking about Work Scrip, it's such a simple way of having a type of money with all its convenience for exchange and economic life yet with none of the drawbacks of encouraging and permitting racketeers that it makes you wonder why people didn't think of it before."

Max looked puzzled. "Racketeers? What are they when they're out?"

"I apologise, I'm interested in twentieth century history, sometimes I get carried away and start imagining that I'm living then."

Max looked shocked, "What the hell would you want to do that for?"

I felt myself going red in the face, "Don't worry, Max, we're all a little eccentric where I come from. But racketeers, there were plenty of them in the old days. Ever hear of a guy called Al Capone?"

"No I can't say I have," Max answered.

"He was a criminal in the USA, that was in the 1920s and 1930s. You know the sort of thing they used to have, pay up or you'll have an accident, selling sex, drugs, booze, that sort of thing."

Max jigged Errico up and down. "I'm with you now."

"Well, Capone once said that he only ran rackets and that there was no difference between him and the regular capitalists; 'business is just the legitimate rackets', he said."

"Now I know where you are," Max exclaimed, "why didn't you just say capitalists, criminals, then I'd have known what you were on about. Racketeers, eh? That's a new one on me."

I pulled a funny face at Errico who obliged me by gurgling, then I took a deep breath and spoke. "Actually, Max, that's what I'm here about. The Eastern Fed have asked me to look into this capitalist business in Grantham and I understand that you're in the know."

Max stared at me. I felt myself going red in the face again. I wasn't doing so good for a hardened private eye, but then I'm not a hardened private eye. What I didn't feel comfortable with was the look of distrust in Max's eyes. That was something you didn't often see. I began to wonder if I was dragging something nasty from the old world into Atopia.

At last Max stopped scrutinising me.

"I knew about the decision to get someone to look for the capitalist. I'm just a little surprised that it's happened I suppose." Max smiled again. "I'm sorry, it's just, you know, who likes to think of anything turning up from the old days? But you're right, I did meet him ..."

"Him?"

"Him. A tall bloke. Old fashioned grey suit, light coloured hair, called himself Carnegie."

"Where did you meet him?"

"Right here, right where you're standing. He was talking a lot of rubbish so I didn't realise who he was until the Angries began to make a noise about him and the implications for Atopia."

"When you say talking a lot of rubbish, what sort of rubbish?" I asked.

"Well, he offered to do a deal with me, said there was profit in it."

"Profit?"

"Yes," Max laughed, "but I'd been drinking and I wasn't sure what he was on about. Said with his help I could make a killing on my trading down in Kent. But how, don't ask me, what with his strange language and the beer I'd drunk it was all a little hazy. Anyway, he went off eventually and I've not seen him since."

"When was this?" I asked.

"Three months ago, or perhaps more, I can't remember. It didn't seem important at the time."

"Do you know if anyone else saw him?"

"This came up at local meetings, and at the Fed's big meeting, but it looks as if I was the last to see him, in Grantham at least."

"Did he say where he was going?"

Max shook his head. "If he did I can't remember, I'm sorry."

"Max, Max! Come and join us for a game!" A tall thin woman stood by the cyberboard calling Max over. Max nodded to her, apologised to me and said he see me later. He and Errico went off for a cyberbout.

If Max was right, and I didn't see why he shouldn't be, I had come to a dead end hardly before I'd started. I was looking for a grey-suited man with light hair called Carnegie, or perhaps he wasn't by now. Where he'd gone and what he was up to I didn't know, and it didn't look as if I was going to find out. I stared into the bottom of my glass and felt bad. A hand touched me on the shoulder and I turned to see the young concrete-shoveller in the jeans that fitted. Suddenly I didn't feel so bad.

4.
Cobblers and Co-ops

Fitted jeans had left early and only the slight aftertaste of sex, beer and concrete remained. I lay in the narrow, messed-up bed and watched the dust rise in the shafts of early sunlight. I hadn't got too far and it didn't look as if I was going to get any further at the moment. I closed my eyes and reviewed the case. There wasn't much to review. The capitalist was a man, a man in a grey suit calling himself Carnegie, at least he was when he was last heard of. That was something like three months ago when he left Grantham. Max had made some more enquiries among his regulars, but no one had any idea where he'd gone. All that was certain was that he wasn't in Grantham, and that was about it. Perhaps it was a good job that I hadn't lived in twentieth century LA, I wouldn't have lasted long. It'd have been the soup kitchen and the hobo jungle for me, or maybe something worse like becoming a Hollywood starlet. I should have been so lucky.

I stayed long enough at The Woolpack to give Max a hand with his computer, clean a few rooms and prepare a few meals. After that I said my farewells and left the Black Banner town. It was Max who'd given me the idea. Why not try Lincoln, he'd suggested. That was where the Angries were making the most noise, perhaps the capitalist was in Lincoln. I couldn't think of a better idea, so I took the train to the city, after hot-faxing the Eastern Fed telling them how I was getting on. It was a short hot-fax.

* * *

Lincoln's a town with a split personality, or it must have been in the past. The cathedral and the old town perched on the great rock outcrop that dominates the country for miles around, and commercial Lincoln spread out beneath the sacred and pretty town on the hill. But developments in Atopia had changed that, for the old town was no longer full of antique shops, solicitors and the well-heeled. Small workshops and repair centres had infiltrated it and it was as busy as the rest of Lincoln, and no longer just with old-style tourists.

I wandered slowly up towards the cathedral thinking that I had a real problem on my hands. How the hell was I going to find out what the Angries were up to? They were so bloody secretive, like any cult. And how would that help me find the capitalist, if he was still in town? I needed an ally, or at the least I needed an informant. But that was another concept that had gone with the past.

I left my bag at a Wanderer's hostel, then went for a walk around the old town. It didn't take long, the keen wind and the rain driving me quickly around the streets and the cathedral. Like most of the old religious sites it was inhabited by small groups of theists belonging to dozens of little cults, and secular groups like the Angries. In a way it's strange that they should live side-by-side, theists and atheists. But they had one thing in common, something that they recognise I suppose. They were all living in another world, be it christian heaven or a workers' state. The poor dupes didn't realise that we'd already found it, or as much as we could get of it at the moment. Heaven that is. Atopia.

My wanderings had got me wet and brought me to a shop window full of shoes, boots and books, all thrown together in a great heap. A sign hanging over the door read 'Albert Lenantais – Cobbler'. I pushed open the door and went in.

You get the impression that cobblers' shops are one of the unchanging things in life. They always smell the same – glue, friction-burnt leather, mixed with the second-hand warmth of countless feet. Complementing it all there's usually a small ageless cobbler with half-moon glasses and a stoop. Albert Lenantais didn't disappoint. Before the bell on the door had stopped ringing a small dark-featured, grey-haired man appeared from the depths of the workshop. He stopped under a sing that swung from the roof announcing 'NEITHER GOD NOR MASTER'. I nodded at the sign, "A bit old fashioned isn't it?"

He laughed. "Not when you get the cathedral mob dropping in to get their shoes fixed." He laughed again, "they still haven't got used to Atopia, it still irritates them." He looked me over. "You look wet, come through the back and get dry."

I walked under the old anarchist slogan and followed the cobbler.

Neither god nor master. The old ones are the best.

The back of the workshop was close and cramped, the small room containing a bed, a stove and walls that groaned with books.

"You deal in books as well, Lenantais?" I asked.

"Call me Albert." He pronounced it the French way. "No I'm a collector. If you've got anything I'm interested in I'll fix your shoes for a swap. Here, give me your jacket."

I took my jacket off and he hung it by the stove. He seemed to be a collector of old anarchist propaganda and writings, pre-utopian stuff. He had an interesting library. A nicely-bound copy of *News From Nowhere* lay on a little table near me.

"You've got some good stuff here, Albert."

"I should have, forty years of collecting." He reached over his bed and pulled an old leather-bound book from a sagging shelf that looked as if it made sleeping a dangerous affair.

"Yes, forty years of collecting, look at this for example."

I took the book and read the embossed title on the cover, *Various Broadsides and Sallies Attributed to Gerrard Winstanley*. I looked up at Lenantais.

"Of course the binding's much later, eighteenth century, but it's the real McCoy. And there's a few things in there that you won't find in the current editions."

The old cobbler took the book back and silently gazed at the *Broadsides and Sallies*. "Winstanley" he murmured, "he was the man, 'as long as such are Rulers as call Land theirs, upholding this particular propriety of Mine and Thine; the common people shall never have their liberty, nor the Land ever be freed from troubles, oppression and complainings'," he quoted.

"But it took us long enough to listen to the Winstanleys," I said.

Lenantais laughed, "but we did and the four hundred years wait means that there's plenty in the way of old books and pamphlets for a nut like me to collect. You'd be surprised at the number of folks who were talking anarchy, talking utopias."

I nodded. "Yes, I've read a little myself. I like to think I'm a bit of an historian of the old times."

"An historian, eh?" Lenantais grinned broadly. "I can feel a good afternoon's talk coming on here, wait a minute."

Lenantais went back into the shop and I heard him pulling the blind down on the door, then he came back. "That'll keep them out. Coffee, or a glass of Imp's Ale?"

"The Imp's Ale will do me fine."

"Wise woman. Anyway, I've not much coffee left. It's not easy to get. But the Imp's Ale is the best."

Lenantais stuffed a couple of logs into the stove, sending sparks flying around my feet, then he rummaged under his bed, eventually pulling out half a crate of beer. "This should do us," he mumbled to himself.

Fortunately the cobbler seemed to be immune to the power of Imp's Ale and drank most of the crate. I only took three bottles, but I could feel my head swimming by the time it began to get dark outside. Or perhaps it was Lenantais' encyclopaedic knowledge of old anarchist writings. Some way into the second bottle I began to think that I'd made a mistake in dropping into the little cobbler's shop in the shadow of the cathedral. And what was worse, I couldn't see a way of introducing the real reason for my visit into the conversation. Lenantais seemed to be so otherworldly with his talk of different editions, textual flaws and disputed authorship that I couldn't see how to tell him that I was on the trail of a capitalist, or that the Angries might be getting dangerous.

But Lenantais solved the problem for me.

"I've a silly question for you, Albert," I said in one of the pauses in his historical-literary monologue brought about by his struggling with another bottle.

"Go ahead." He waved his free hand. "Go ahead. Silly questions are my speciality."

"Why the name? I don't recognise Albert Lenantais from any heroes of the old days."

"Ah, '1927 – the Vegan centre and the Anarchists' not mean anything to you?"

"Not a thing, Albert, not a thing."

"Léo Malet?"

I shook my head.

"Well, Léo Malet was a French singer and anarchist writer. He wrote dozens of rather poor books about a character called Nestor Burma.

One of them is called *Fog on the Tolbiac Bridge* and the story centres on a bunch of anarchists that hung out in a vegan centre in 1920s Paris. Nestor Burma is one of them and years later he finds that most of the others fell by the wayside when it came to their commitment to anarchy. All except Albert Lenantais, that is. Only he's murdered."

"Murdered?"

The cobbler laughed, "Yes, folk used to really go for books like that in the old days, you see, this Nestor Burma chap was what was called a private detective."

"Tell me about it!" I laughed.

After that it was easy. I managed to stop Lenantais giving me a history of detective fiction and got him focused on my case instead. The old boy wasn't surprised that the Eastern Fed was getting a bit worried about the idea of a capitalist giving the Angries an opening to talk about weapons and fighting, in fact Lenantais had noticed that the Angries had seemed more fanatical than usual. They'd taken to quoting Trotsky's and Lenin's dictums from the period of the Russian Civil War, the first one that is. All the usual stuff about discipline and vengeance.

"I had one of the Angries in here on Tuesday. Decent sort of bloke, he is. He's only been with them for two years so he'd still what the Angries call a 'revolutionary novice', that's the lowest grade they have" Lenantais explained.

"Grade?"

"Yes", he laughed, "they have a whole system of grades from novices to 'Archproletarian'. All to do with their obsession about 'revolutionary discipline'. Anyway this chap started quoting a Leninist newspaper from the period when that woman Fania Kaplan tried to bump Lenin off: 'We will kill our enemies in scores of hundreds, let them be thousands, let them drown themselves in their own blood, let there be floods of blood of the bourgeoisie, more blood, as much as possible'. That sort of thing, you know, authoritarian statist insanity." Albert shrugged his shoulders and looked at me sadly.

"And you say they've only recently started to talk like this?"

"Yes. It's normally quotes about how Lenin was 'as mighty as the ocean, as tender as the southern sun', that sort of thing. But now you've told me about this bloody capitalist wandering about I can see what's got into them. They're getting all apocalyptical, it'll be the second coming of Trot soon. Daft buggers."

Albert's news cleared the fuzz of Imp's Ale from my mind. It suddenly seemed to be much more serious than either I or the Fed had thought. It looked as if it might be a race against time. I needed to find this capitalist, Carnegie, fast, and I had to find out just what he was playing at.

"Albert, I need your help. For the first time since I set out from Oxford I feel that there might really be something nasty happening in Atopia. Until I heard your news I suppose I thought the whole thing was a bit of a joke – I mean, a capitalist in Atopia! But there might well be something in the Angries connection. If they really are thinking about 'blood and more blood' because of this capitalist, then I've got to find him, and quick. And I've got to admit that I've very little idea where I can find him, but it may be that the Angries know. So, I need to get among the Angries. But I've no contacts here, except you."

The cobbler stared at me over the rim of his glasses, his eyes both sad and empty. Was that because of the half-crate of Imp's Ale or was it some vague perception of the re-emergence of conflict and killing, capitalism and statism? Was Lenantais' historical imagination conjuring up ancient demons to pollute the balance and harmony of Atopia?

"How can I help? Man, I'm just an old book-collecting cobbler," he said.

"But you know some Angries from the cathedral, you've said so."

"Yes, they come in here, get their boots repaired, preach to me from their texts, but that's it. I'm not interested in them or in their insular little life, and they're certainly not interested in me, one of the unelect, a reformist, a trade unionist or whatever else they think I am, along with the rest of the population."

It occurred to me that Lenantais was scared, that the talk of blood and war had frightened him. I wasn't surprised, it frightened me. The first signs of a social disease, all from the rumour of capitalism. But I had to get the old man to help, he was my only contact in Lincoln, and I didn't think that I had time to look for other help.

"Albert, you've got to help. This could be a big thing, you realise that, I can see. Okay, you aren't close to the Angries, but you know more about them than I do. You must have some contact, some knowledge that would enable me to get among them, find out what's going on. Please, Albert, this might be critical for Atopia. Hell, you don't want to go back to the past, do you? Death, suffering, competition, hatreds, fear, and a few Winstanleys talking to themselves?"

The mention of Gerrard Winstanley seemed to do the trick. Perhaps Lenantais imagined the world turned upside down again, but, this time, it would be the wrong way.

"You're right. But I still don't see ..." he stopped, took a swig from his glass and sat still, tasting the ale. "I think I may know just the man you're looking for. He's a bloke named Jack Jackson and he's a member of the 'Green England Co-op'. You might have noticed it coming into Lincoln on the train, big green and brown painted place surrounded by allotments, green, white and red flag flying over it. Anyway, Jack might be your man."

"How's that? Surely he's not an Angry if he's actually involved in producing something?"

"No he's not an Angry himself, but he's in love with one of them. Or perhaps I should say he's fixated by one of them, beautiful red-haired woman named Beatrice. But you know how they are, don't like their people having sex with the rest of us, so poor old Jack hangs around their meetings making cow-eyes at Beatrice. He's been doing it for so long that they've got used to him. So, he might be your man. I'll give you a note saying I've sent you."

"That's great. Thanks, Albert."

"No thanks needed, you know that." The old man grinned, finished his beer and began to root about for writing paper and a pencil.

*   *   *

Lenantais had wanted me to stay the night. I was grateful for his help, but not that grateful. I stayed to down a few more bottles and eat with him. After a goodbye kiss I left him and stumbled back to the Wanderer's Hostel. Next morning I was up early, ate a hearty breakfast of bacon, black pudding and toast and headed out to the 'Green England Co-Op'.

These co-ops keep the old name of Atopia – England – as a reminder that they'd helped to lead the way to Atopia before most other groups, even most anarchists. They'd started out as local co-ops organised by disillusioned Green Party activists who'd got fed up with the political careerism of their leaders, and wanted to do something more immediate and positive in their quest for an ecologically sound world. They'd started by repairing goods that had been made with the principle of in-built obsolescence in mind. In the days of capitalist mass consumption practically nothing could be repaired unless it was sent back to the manufacturers, except that they didn't repair anything, they only wanted to sell you a new one. But the Green England people decided to break that cycle of waste and set up local co-ops designed to repair anything from a hairdryer on up. They also built up a national information network of obsolete spare parts. Needless to say the big manufacturers weren't very happy about all this and tried to close the Green England people down. But the law of property didn't work very well for the big boys – just for a change. There were too many of these little co-ops repairing and even doing a little manufacturing in their own right. And the mass unemployment and poverty of so many people in the early 21st century meant that the Green Englands flourished, as they would barter as well as sell their services. They even became fashionable among those with money – 'chic' was the word, I think.

* * *

The road to the co-op was bounded on both sides by allotments, green in places with the remains of winter crops, and brown with the neatly prepared ground ready for spring sowings. A group of tall women were flinging turnips into the back of a cart drawn up at the roadside. They smiled and shouted 'hello' as I passed, and I caught one of them commenting 'nice bum' as she hefted another handful of turnips.

The co-op itself was painted green and brown to match the allotments. I crossed over the light railway tracks that ran to the side of the long building and entered 'Door A'. An old man was sitting just inside the door in a deep, high-backed armchair, drinking from a large mug, his feet on a desk marked 'INFORMATION' and his free hand stroking the back of a contented black and white cocker spaniel.

"Hiya, what can I do for you this morning?"

"Hello. My name's Anne. I'm looking for a member of your co-op, a man called Jack Jackson."

"Yeah, I know the fella. Fancy a cup of tea?"

"No thanks, I've not long had breakfast."

"You new round here, Anne?"

"Yes. About Jack ..."

"What would you be wanting him for? Romantic interest, eh?"

"Not that I know of. Albert Lenantais sent me."

"Why didn't you say before?" He took his feet off the desk and sat up. "I know Albert. Damn fine cobbler, fix anything. You know, I had a pair of ..."

I began to think that I'd get more sense out of the cocker spaniel. "Jack Jackson, where can I find him?"

My tormentor laughed. "Through there," he pointed, "in the main workshop. But there ain't no hurry, they're having the day's meeting."

"Thanks." I grinned. "Perhaps I'll take you up on that cup of tea when I've seen Jack."

"Sure, it'll be waiting for you, Anne."

*   *   *

I pushed through the double doors at the end of the corridor and entered the main workshop, a large, light-filled shed with work benches and machine tools ringing the co-op's daily meeting. The co-op members were listening to a small bespectacled man in green overalls giving what appeared to be an account of the stocks of sheet metal of various gauges that they had in hand. A young girl of about thirteen interrupted him to ask a question about the quality of metal that they'd taken recently from some other co-op. This started a general discussion, and I took the opportunity to quietly join the meeting, taking a stool at the back. After about ten minutes on the quality issued, the stock report was resumed. A vote was taken at the end of it and then the meeting broke up as the co-op members wandered off, some to the work benches and others to the doors that I'd entered through, perhaps to the allotments or maybe just home.

The girl that had spoken about the sheet metal quality came over to me, smiling. Close to she looked as if she might be older than thirteen, but not much. She had a small face with delicate features and brown straight hair, she was dressed in tight yellow overalls and long green boots.

"Hi, I'm Aphrodite, welcome to Green England."

"Aphrodite? She wasn't English was she?"

The girl grinned. "Who cares? I like the name. How about you?"

"Yes, I like it, it suits you."

She liked the compliment and her smile grew even wider.

"And yours?"

"Anne, Anne Riorden."

"That's okay, but it's not really in the same league as Aphrodite, is it?"

"You're right there, sister. But how about Jack Jackson, have you heard that name?"

"Have I? He works with me. Do you want to speak to him?"

I nodded.

"This way."

I followed Aphrodite across the workshop to an L-shaped bench in the far corner. A round-shouldered, red-haired, middle-aged bloke was tinkering with a very small electric motor. He looked up as we approached.

"Jack, I've someone to see you," Aphrodite said.

I stepped forward and held out my hand. "Hi, I'm Anne Riorden."

"Jack Jackson." He let go of my hand and picked up the motor again. "We get them from a group in the west midlands, but sometimes their quality control isn't what it should be."

"Like with the metal sheeting?"

"What? Oh, you heard the discussion at the meeting. No, that's just Aphrodite here being finicky."

The girl laughed. "Perfection is my guide, as William Morris said."

"Did he?" I asked.

She grinned. "Who cares?"

I grinned back, then turned to Jack who'd looked as if his concern for the motor was going to absorb all his attention before I'd got the chance to ask him about the Angries.

"Jack, I've got a letter here from Albert Lenantais, I'd like to talk to you about it. Do you have fifteen minutes to spare?"

"Sure he does," Aphrodite said. "I'll look after your little motor, Jack." She took the motor from him and sat at the bench.

Jack looked at me as if to say 'Kids!'

"Looks as if I do have fifteen minutes."

We walked slowly through the workshops and out into the allotments, Jack telling me about the work and organisation of the place. Because the co-op's roots lay in the old ecological movement, especially the Green Party, they had a more structured way of organising themselves than I was used to at Oxford. All the members of the co-op could turn their hand to any of the tasks that the co-op undertook, although there were specialists that tended to do particular tasks. As well as working in the co-op itself, each member had an allotment which they worked themselves and, in addition, any member could do whatever else they felt like provided they put in fifteen hours a week on the main business of the co-op, which was light engineering work. Most of the work was on the repair and reconditioning of a variety of machinery and white electrical goods. But they also ran a small production facility that produced washing machines. This provided the co-op with goods that they could put in one of Lincoln's communal depots and, in return, they could take other goods from the depot. They did all of the assembly work on the washing machines at the co-op, although they didn't make the motors or some semi-finished materials which they bartered with other co-ops, less formal groups and even one-person enterprises primarily in the west midlands. The whole thing was run by a members' forum elected on a monthly basis by all members, while a daily meeting was held to discuss any matters that arose as well as being empowered to dismiss the members' forum and call a new election before the fixed monthly date. In this way over a hundred members controlled their own productive endeavours.

*   *   *

Jack took me to his own allotment and fixed me a cup of tea on the stove in his shed. We sat on a heavily patched sofa, and I enjoyed the tea while Jack read the letter that Lenantais had written. It was a long letter, the old cobbler having given chapter and verse of the whole situation as I'd explained it, and his own theories about the last capitalist, amply illustrated by quotations from half-forgotten anarchist writings. I was pouring myself a second cup when Jack finished.

"So you want me to introduce you to some Angries?"

"Well, not necessarily introduce me, just get me into one of their meetings without making too much of a fuss, you know, I don't really want the whole evangelical treatment, I'd just like to listen, see where they're at, see if they have any idea where the capitalist is."

He looked at me thoughtfully, his pale face tense under the unruly mess of his red hair. "Is it really as serious as Albert makes out?" he asked, waving the letter.

"Well, that's what I want to find out, but from what Albert tells me it could be. In any event, I think it might be an idea to find this capitalist."

"Is that your main task?"

"Yes."

"But what about the Angries?"

"Well, they're important, but only because of the capitalist. If I can find him then we'll be able to lay all the rumours to rest and then the Angries won't be able to say that Atopia is really a bourgeois society, or whatever, and we can all go back to normal. And there won't be any guns. If I find the capitalist."

Jack smiled. "Well, that might be easier than you think. He's in Sheffield."

5.
Man in a Red Windsor Tie

Outside the central station in Sheffield – John Elliot Station, named after one of the many navvies killed building the old Woodhead Tunnel in the 1840s – there is a small garden planted with evergreen trees and bushes. The trams run noisily round this little garden, but as the sun was shining I decided that it would be a good place to eat my sandwiches. I dodged between trams and opened the gate into the garden, found a tree stump to sit on, opened my sandwiches and began to think over the information that Jack Jackson had given me. He'd met the capitalist at a meeting of the co-op over a month ago, when a man in a grey suit had asked permission to speak on an 'issue that would benefit them all'. The man had introduced himself as Henry Frick, and had begun to talk to the co-op members about the necessity of product diversification and the need for constantly changing new lines, advertising and bartering the allotment land away. Jack had said that it was a while before any of them could really make much of what Frick was going on about as he used so many archaic phrases, but once they'd got his general drift they'd just put him down as a harmless nut and ended the meeting. Frick had buttonholed Jack afterwards and told him that he was on a country-wide tour trying to convince people of the need for new methods, and that Sheffield was his next stop. Jack's opinion was that Frick should have stayed put in the cathedral among the other proselytising nutters. Although Jack's capitalist called himself Frick, I was pretty sure than it was the same guy who had called himself Carnegie before. Jack's description of him as a grey man in a grey suit fitted. Now I had to find him in Sheffield.

*   *   *

In the corner of the little garden was a statue of two women. I went over, munching my last beef and onion sandwich, and read the inscription on the plinth. It was to the memory of two members of the All Asian Women's League who had been killed in Sheffield by religious fundamentalists. The later years of the old system had seen the rise of fundamentalist religion throughout the country, with the christian 'House' movement taking on a new and dangerously aggressive evangelical streak, something that was mirrored by other groups such as sections of the islamic community. In retrospect we can see that this period marked the swan-song of religion in a period of economic and social crisis, but at the time it looked like a groundswell reaction to the libertarian experiments that were beginning to change the country and lead to the creation of Atopia. One of the leading groups in both the defeat of organised religion and the opening of Atopia was the All Asian Women's League, who campaigned for the full rights of women from the islamic communities to determine the shape of their own lives free from the constraints of religious faith. Many women had suffered in that struggle, being shunned by their communities, ignored by the old political groupings afraid of losing electoral support, and being physically attacked by fanatics. The two women commemorated by the statue in Sheffield had been assassinated by gunmen hired by religious leaders in Yorkshire. But their deaths, and those of other members of AAWL, had helped tip the balance against religion. And the identification of other non-islamic communities with the demands for harsher laws against apostates meant that religion as a major social force was finally finished, while the entire network of local anti-religious groups, like AAWL, built on an autonomous form of organisation, provided continued self-help support for other struggles in the long move to Atopia.

*   *   *

I was still standing at the foot of the statue wishing that I had some flowers to put with the other bouquets, both fresh and withered, that lay around the plinth, when I suddenly got the feeling that someone was watching me. I wheeled around quickly and saw a man was standing a few yards behind me chewing on a cigarette that had gone out. I was surprised that he'd managed to get so close to me without my hearing him, as he was thick-set and heavy in build. But what startled me even more was that he was wearing an old-fashioned twentieth century suit in crumpled grey wool. He even wore a grey shirt and his face was greyish too, although he had a crimson tie around his neck. A quotation came to mind: 'His face was broad, thick-featured and intelligent. For colour he depended on a red windsor tie that blossomed over his grey flannel shirt'. That was from one of my favourite detective novels from the 1920s, *Red Harvest* by an American writer with the right sympathies, Dashiell Hammet. In the book the grey man with the red tie is a rather ambiguous Wobbly organiser called Bill Quint, but now I wondered if my man in a grey suit with the red windsor tie was Frick, or Carnegie, or whoever.

Red tie grinned. "Sorry, did I startle you?"

"You did."

"Sorry."

"You said that."

"Well I am. I didn't want to interrupt you. You seemed pretty deep in thought."

"Yes." I smiled. "Yes, you're right, I was." I waved my hand at the statue. "Brave women. I was just thinking how much of a struggle it was for people to create a different world and how terrible if we were to see any of the old ways return."

He laughed, white teeth flashing in his greyish face. "Why should they?"

That was the sort of reply I'd hoped for. I supposed that the capitalist would have been only too keen to take the opportunity to defend the old ways.

"My name's Anne Riorden." I held out my hand.

Red tie stepped forward and shook hands. "Pleased to meet you, the name's Saffo." He nodded in the direction of my bag. "You new in town?"

"Yes, I've just got in from Lincoln. I'm looking for a man, actually." I thought I'd try a different approach for a change.

He grinned. "Anyone in particular?"

"Yes, I'm afraid so. He goes by the name of Henry Frick, or perhaps Carnegie, probably Andrew Carnegie."

Saffo shook his head. "Never heard of the guy, and I get around. Has he been in Sheffield long?"

"Certainly no more than a month, maybe less."

"Why are you looking for him?"

"It's a long story."

"I've got time, who hasn't? Fancy a cup of tea, and you can tell me about it?"

Saffo seemed to be a bright sort of guy and I remembered the role of the Wobbly with the red tie in *Red Harvest*, so we went to a café across the road and up the hill from the two heroines in stone.

A yellow and black sign announced that the café was run by the Sheffield Central Association, providing basic meals for free to all Sheffield inhabitants. As I wasn't from Sheffield I offered Eastern Scrip, which they took. I could have passed myself off as a Sheffielder, but why? Saffo and I took seats by the window and basked in the warm spring sunlight.

"What's the Sheffield Central Association?" I asked.

"Oh Sheffield's pretty formally run. The whole city's divided into different areas, some of them fairly small, maybe a dozen or so streets and a few workshops, but all negotiated and negotiable by the people who live in each area. The basic communal activities are run by each area, each Association, so they sort out their own services, like this café. They also negotiate their dealings with other Associations. I live in the Crooksmoor Association, so I do various jobs and tasks there, as well as pursuing my main interest in education."

"Anything in particular?"

"Literature and some language teaching, Russian and French. The steel and engineering co-ops retain me to help facilitate classes for their members. You know, I just visit the various education centres and act as a resource, although sometimes they want to give me more formal sort of help, the odd talk now and then – the usual stuff, you know. It's a good set-up here in Sheffield, the steel and engineering co-ops are co-ordinated by a Producers' Council, they're responsible for our trade beyond Sheffield and our working alliances with people like the Humberside Shipping Association, getting our stuff further abroad, that sort of thing."

"Sounds a bit bureaucratic. Is it?"

"No, not in the sense that we have regular pen-pushers. It's like everything else, turn and turn about, along with regular meetings and no re-election clauses. I've even done some time on the Producers' Council myself a few years back, helped arrange for a big barter job with engine builders in the Baltic, as well as doing work with the

Education Committee. All the co-ordination stuff's important, with so many small workshops, and even the two bigger mills depend on the smaller co-ops for specialist materials. Got to keep everyone sweet. It's difficult sometimes, this being Yorkshire, but with us all having the tendency to co-operation, well, you know ..."

Saffo swallowed some of his tea and bit into his bacon roll.

"Yes, it's strange to think that the dominant ideology was once competition and 'bugger thy neighbour'. Co-operation's the best way to run our lives, but sometimes I think that perhaps it's a fragile utopia."

Saffo looked up from his roll. "In what way?"

"It wouldn't take too much to upset the whole thing, the whole balance of our society."

He shook his big head. "I don't agree with you there. Things change, of course they do, that's the nature of society, evolution through co-operation, you know. But all our freedoms have been too hard won for people to want to give them up. Why give up something that works, something that guarantees peace, provides you with a varied and secure life?"

"Ever heard of the old saying about barrels and rotten apples?" I asked.

"Can't say I have. Is the idea that one apple'll spoil the rest?"

"Got it in one."

"So where's the bad apple?" Saffo swept his hand around, indicating the laughing child and the old woman who were dispensing the food behind the counter, and the mix of quiet but relaxed people eating and chatting.

"Remember in the garden I said I was looking for a bloke named Frick or Carnegie?"

"Yes."

"Well, he's a capitalist and he's been responsible for raising trouble from Grantham to Lincoln, and perhaps right through the Eastern Fed. I'm here on behalf of the Fed to find him and find out what he thinks he's playing at."

Saffo sat still for a few moments, letting my information sink in, then he said "A capitalist? What for? Why?"

"Like I said, that's why I'm here, to find out. And time may be running short because the Angries have decided that the existence of this guy, or maybe more than one man, proves that Atopia isn't a workers' state."

Saffo butted in with a harsh laugh. "It isn't any sort of state!"

"Right, but the Angries think our roving capitalist is the final proof they need that the revolution is on its way."

Saffo shook his head. "I never did understand those guys, we've had the revolution and we didn't shed one drop of blood, just contracted other ways of doing things, like Landauer said. But empirical reality never did dent some people's faith." He took another bite of his bacon roll and spoke with his mouth full. "I don't like the sound of all this. You need to find this guy quick."

"I know, and I'm not doing a very good job."

"What you need is to talk to the City Association. There's a meeting tonight. I'll take you. They'll find out where your Mr Frick's got to, someone will know."

*   *   *

The thrice-weekly City Association meeting was packed as it was a transference meeting when the new committee, elected the day before in the usual electronic election by all the people of Sheffield, took over from the old committee for the first of its fifteen sessions before the next election. Saffo knew most of the people there and took me round several of them before the general consensus emerged that I should address the whole meeting about the problem. I wasn't too keen on this as I felt that the whole thing would get out and might aid the purposes of both Frick and the Angries by panicking people. I got short shrift with that argument, and I felt a little stupid when it was pointed out that what I was asking for was some kind of secrecy, keeping information from the people that had a right to know – everyone. Not for the first time I began to wonder if the case was beginning to taint my judgement and that the mere presence of the capitalist, and my preoccupation with him, was beginning to infect me with the virus of the old days. I hoped it wasn't and that the capitalist wasn't having an effect like that on others.

I addressed the meeting and got what I wanted. A small, dark-haired independent woman producer and steel worker, called Louise, had met the capitalist, only this time he was calling himself Nuffield – he certainly had a sense of history. He'd wanted to use her contacts with independent producers to set up a 'deal',as he called it, with other producers outside Sheffield, mainly with agricultural producers in the Snowdonia area. That had sounded okay to Louise, but then he'd said that he would do all the contact work and would expect a large chunk of the produce for his services. She'd told him to jump, the idea had seemed so silly. I agreed, but it was a pity she hadn't found out where in Snowdonia, or even if he was going there. Anyway, it was clear that I had to go to Wales.

6.
A Hill in Wales

'The proletariat, betraying its instincts, despising its historic mission, has let itself be perverted by the dogma of work. Rude and terrible has been its punishment. All its individual and social woes are born of its passion for work.' The train carriage taking me towards Snowdonia was decorated inside like a giant newspaper or book with quotations from Paul Lafargue's marvellous booklet *The Right to be Lazy*. Between the columns of 'print' on the carriage walls there were paintings illustrating the horrors of wage slavery in the years prior to the establishment of Atopia, along with the ironic presentation of old leftist slogans associated with demands for more wage slavery. I've always liked Lafargue's booklet, as much for its humour as its critique of capitalism. I searched around the carriage until I found my favourite quotation arranged around the luggage racks: 'Jehovah the bearded and angry god, gave his worshippers the supreme example of ideal laziness; after six days of work, he rests for all eternity.' All that reading, and the thought of my quest for Nuffield, or Carnegie, Frick or whatever he was calling himself at the moment, tired me out. I could have done with a few slugs from a half pint bottle of bourbon, like the shamuses in the old days, but I don't like the stuff. So I contented myself with a bottle of Sheffield Famous Black Porter and promptly fell asleep under Lafargue's admonitions to be lazy.

*   *   *

The first thing that struck me about the Snowdonia region was how heavily populated it was. That was going to make it difficult to find the capitalist, if he was in the area at all. I took a motorbike from the station transport pool and signed a book to say that I would return it to a station in Wales within the month.

The motorbike took me round the towns and villages in a light haze of wood alcohol fumes. Its speed and mobility enabled me to get a good picture of the area, and ask at dozens of pubs about the capitalist. But, after a week I had found nothing and I was getting

tired. It looked as if the trail had run cold. I hot-faxed the Eastern
Fed, telling them of my troubles, and saying that I'd stay on the case
for another few days and then give up. But once I'd sent the hot-fax
I felt bad, 'giving up' didn't feel right. I wasn't the only one involved
in all this. And, anyway, who ever heard of Lew Archer or Philip
Marlowe 'giving up'? They hung in there even when their half-guilty
clients tried to pay them off. I decided I couldn't let Lew and Philip
down. I got back on the bike and burnt up a few more miles up and
down the tree-covered hills and mountains.

I chugged slowly up towards the top of the steep mountain roadway,
singing an old song at the top of my voice – 'You don't want me, that's
why I'm going home ...' – although my voice doesn't have the right
nasal howl. Despite my failure to find the capitalist I felt good, the
clean sharp air of the mountains carrying with it the tang of the sea
had buoyed me up. It had been raining, heavy swift-running spring
rain that came out of a seeming clear sky, but now the sun was
raising steam from the blacktop. The mixed woodland that covered
the top of the hills and mountains was alive with bird life, stunned
into song by the sudden spring shower, the pines spread their tangy
scent and the birch and beech were beginning to show green buds.
The bike crested the mountain top and I began the long twisting
descent into the valley below.

About seven hundred feet below the woodland petered out and the
first of the valley floor farms and workshops appeared, mixed with
coppices of willows and poplars. Cattle and a few sheep grazed in
some of the fields, while pigs rooted among the remains of the winter
crops. A timber mill stood by a junction, bracketed by tall windtowers.
The mill was hung with a signpost that announced that it was also a
wanderer's hostel. I'd been riding since early that morning and I was
feeling hungry, and this was the beginning of yet another heavily
populated valley that I should check out.

I propped the bike outside the long, low building that was the hostel,
unstrapped my bag, and took it in with me. It was quiet inside,
although I could hear the sound of someone whistling in the distance.
Like most of the modern buildings, the hostel was built of wood, and
the air was warm with the smell of the sun on wooden walls. I decided
to attract some attention to myself.

"Hello! Hello! Anyone alive?"

There was a stirring in the far corner of the refectory, and I noticed for the first time that a hammock was slung in the corner. A bespectacled face surmounted by thick curly hair peered at me over the edge of the hammock.

"Hey, no need to shout, I'd have woken up."

The hammock swung and a tall, dark man in his early thirties leapt down, grinning.

"Eventually," he said.

"Sorry, I didn't see you in the corner."

"That's my lair you know, like a spider, except I'm not quite as active. The name's Bryn, or perhaps it's Trevor." He shook his head. "What day is it?"

"Wednesday."

"Then I'm Bryn, and you are?"

"Anne, Anne Riorden."

"Wanderer?"

"Sort of."

"Well, sort of wanderer, are you looking for a bed or just something to eat?"

"Both, probably."

"Great, we'll start with the food, then we'll see to the bed." He smiled at me with his eyes as well as his mouth, and I began to think that stopping my bike at this particular hostel might have been the best move I'd made all week.

"Take a seat, and I'll fix you something. Bacon and bread do you?"

I sat down at one of the long trestles. "Yes, that'd be fine. Any beer? I'm thirsty."

"Sure thing. Betws-y-coed Best. One bottle or two?"

"Will you join me?"

"Of course."

"Make it two then."

He laughed and disappeared through the swinging doors at the back of the room.

Bryn re-emerged with bacon, bread and beer for both of us, and we sat in silence for a while as we ate. I couldn't decide whether to ask him straight out about the capitalist, or just concentrate on flirting

with him. I didn't really get a chance, for over the light, Burton-style Betws-y-coed Best, Bryn started telling me about life in Wales and how it was so different from pre-utopia days. I'd made the mistake, again, of mentioning that I was interested in history. Still, it gave me plenty of opportunity to gaze into his lovely eyes while he blathered on about land ownership and land use.

Apparently the entire area had been something of a wet desert prior to the establishment of utopia, with a small and dwindling permanent population supported only by state grants for destructive old-style hill farming, and tourism. The tourists had been both welcome and resented as they eroded the cultural unity of communities, and further exacerbated long-term de-population by driving up house prices – that was in the days when even basic needs were bought and sold for profit. I wondered if my capitalist would be in favour of that. So the area in pre-utopian days was ecologically damaged and de-populated, except for shifting crowds of equally destructive sheep and tourists.

But now things were, as I'd seen, quite different. The area supported a large population existing in bilingual harmony, which was the result of economic stability and the universal and personal liberty that characterised life in these utopian days. Old patterns of land usage had disappeared and ecological regeneration had taken place. No longer were the hills and valleys subject to the sort of 'upside down' practice of free-ranging sheep on the high ground and mono-culture forestry in the valleys. Instead the high slopes and peaks were heavily wooded with mixed plantings and the widespread use of native types, such as the Scots Pine. The valleys themselves were given over to a multitude of farming and industrial activities, with mixed farming and forestry-based industry predominating, along with the maintenance of the biomass plantations of willows and poplars. Sheep were still farmed, but in small numbers, and they were not permitted free access to the land. Similarly, as in the rest of utopia, mass tourism was a thing of the past, with the end of wage slavery and the concept of forty-eight weeks work for four weeks holiday. The general slowing of the pace of life meant that there were plenty of wanderers, but their impact, and the free provision of hostels, meant that no longer did Welsh speakers feel culturally threatened as in pre-utopian days.

Bryn's descriptions of life in the hills made him far more animated than I would have suspected when I first saw his easing his way out of the hammock, and I decided that I would have to spend a few days at least in the area. My silly capitalist seemed to be far away, and the urgency that I'd felt in Sheffield had gone. Perhaps it was the effect of the mountain air, perhaps it was something else.

Bryn went for more beer, then began to expound on the history of land ownership in the area. It was a familiar story, but I liked watching him talk, and the beer was relaxing. The great change in rural land ownership had come with the collapse of two central props of the pre-utopian state – the monarchy and the European Union. Spontaneous land agitation had started in Scotland first, where the tradition of land raids had given an extra impetus to land protest in an age of continued mass unemployment and serious urban decay. Successive governments had adopted a policy of ring-fencing areas of serious urban decay (the blight zones), leaving the inhabitants to the mercy of the drug gangs. This was an acceptable policy, and mirrored the activities of private house developers who were building walled housing schemes that were privately policed. This gave some measure of comfort to those in the private estates, but the people trapped in the blight zones had few choices. Travelling had long been outlawed, so those seeking to escape the blight zones began to stage land raids, occupying marginal land and building shanty homes, in some places reviving the 24-hour house tradition. The state, of course, reacted with violence and increased policing, but the frequency of the raids and the cost of policing meant that many land raiders were able to establish themselves successfully in remote areas of Scotland. And the movement spread, with 'The No-Man's Land People' in England being the first to follow the Scots. The English raiders also called themselves 'Lob's Children' and began the practice of raiding land owned by the royal family. This was a stroke of genius, for the monarchy had long been held in contempt by the people, and the police refused to act against raiders on royal land. This final act of contempt for royalty brought about the collapse of the monarchy, the abdication of the king and the widespread occupation of royal land in England, Scotland and Wales. The movement spread, and resistance from private land holding conglomerates was minimal, thanks to the impotence of the European Union.

The decay of the European Union had been something of a surprise for the advocates of statism. But that super-state was defeated by its inherent tendency to acquire more and more functions, or rather by its desire to pass more and more laws. But the widening of the Union to include most of Europe, including Russia, meant that much of its law-making was ineffectual. The peoples of Europe became increasingly aware that in the face of more and more laws from regional governments, national governments and the European government, they had no option but to ignore most of them – thus the state taught the people anarchy. Tax laws were the most annoying, and ordinary people who didn't have access to lawyers and financial consultants learnt that only participation in the non-money economy freed them from successive layers of state taxation. Widespread tax evasion meshed with the spectacular growth of the barter economy to undermine all levels of government. And the habit spread to other areas of life. Governments found themselves in the position of medieval kings who sent inspectors out to assess the taxable populations of villages only to find that their lands were inhabited solely by non-taxable children and animals. So the much-vaunted European Union found that it had become another Holy Roman Empire, to whom everyone paid lip-service, but none paid taxes. And its revenue-raising failure, along with the membership of countries with large agricultural sectors, resulted in the total collapse of its agricultural policy and a dramatic fall in land prices, just as land owners came under pressure from the laid raiders, and the realisation that agri-business had done dramatic ecological damage that only alternative, and ideally small-scale, methods of husbandry could repair.

*   *   *

Three bottles of Betws-y-coed Best, and staring too deeply into Bryn's dark, animated eyes, had driven all thoughts of the capitalist and the Angries from my mind. And I didn't want to hear any more about the development of the forest farm either.

"Bryn, do you do all your sleeping in that hammock, or have you anywhere more comfortable?"

He looked at the hammock, then back to me. Then he smiled. "Well, I do have a nice wide bed."

"Is it far?"

"Just up the hill, you can take me on your bike."

"One ride for another?"

He laughed, and nodded his head. "You're on."

We left the hostel and went up the hill.

*   *   *

A week later I'd decided the trail had, finally, run cold. Bryn had asked all around and, despite the closeness of the community, no one had seen or heard of the capitalist. I'd failed, but perhaps the capitalist had given up too. It was time to get back to Oxford and tell the Eastern Fed what had happened.

I spent a few hours saying goodbye to Bryn, then we rode down to the station, and he waited with me for the train. I picked up the regional newspaper while Bryn checked in the motorbike. Flicking through the paper, a small paragraph caught my eye. It was headed 'An Eccentric in the Republic', and the few lines told me that a man calling himself Alfred Mond had been standing on the prom at Douglas talking about the virtues of monopoly. I was back in business. Next stop, the Isle of Man, otherwise known throughout Atopia as The Republic.

7.
Meet the President

The Liverpool (New Speke) Air Terminal wasn't that busy, with only five passenger airships tethered outside the terminal buildings. A few technicians were about, and there was an airship in its hangar having its engines overhauled. I'd only flown once before, so I wandered around the terminal, nosing in at the different hangars and bits of equipment. I felt a little let down, being a detective in Atopia just wasn't up to being a gumshoe in California in the 1940s. Taking one of the quiet, fairly slow, fat airships on the hop to The Republic wasn't quite the same as waiting for a dreamboat of a pilot to fly me over the high sierra in a sleek, fast and loud Lockheed Constellation. The golden age of air travel was certainly dead, but then so was crime.

Once, international air travel had been a huge concern swallowing vast amounts of resources, and moving countless millions of people around the world for all sorts of inane reasons. However, the decline of international trade and the astronomical rises in fuel costs signalled the end of large-scale international air travel, even before the establishment of utopian societies throughout the world. Business travellers had been the largest users of air travel, and their abandonment of air lines meant that tourist travel alone was not sufficient to sustain the highly expensive aircraft. These pre-utopian tendencies had, of course, been confirmed by the development of the differing worldwide utopias, of which Atopia was only one, even if it had been one of the first.

The decline of international trade had been a product of the economic collapse of much of the first world. Although the trading system had for centuries been in the hands of the first world, the structural imbalances in those economies meant that smaller and smaller sections of their societies actually benefited from the exploitative gains of the elites. In consequence, the mass of consumers in the first world were unable to purchase the products of worldwide capitalism, just as the workers who produced much of that output in the third world were unable either to purchase their product. Elite consumption was not enough, and there were fewer and fewer new areas open to exploitation. In those countries where some semblance of liberal parliamentary control remained, increasing political pressures meant that certain national states were forced to withdraw from the international trading system. In other areas, most notably in Africa and to a lesser extent in India, individuals and communities realised that their only hope for survival was a complete return to localised economic activity and strategies for survival that were tailored to their specific needs. This movement spread to the first world, providing a timely alternative to the depredations of the international trading system and the increased concentration of economic and political power that went with it. All of these tendencies, of course, but particularly the creation of alternative strategies for life, helped the growth of utopianism worldwide.

The desire of people to avoid government and all its works helped bring about the realisation that only a change of heart could usher in utopia. And, just as the statists saw the wage slaves on which they built their power begin to slip from their grasp, so ecological problems and the failure of key resources brought additional pressures that were, in pre-utopian terms, beyond their ability to tackle successfully. First amongst these resource crises was, of course, the final failure of workable oil fields which cut the technology of power from beneath the feet of the powerful.

*   *   *

It was getting near to embarkation time, so I wandered back to the terminal and confirmed that I would be flying. I had my bag weighed then took it out to Ship 5. The airship was a smooth, hard-shelled balloon of helium, beneath which was suspended a long passenger cabin. Two wide airscrews projected from the engines at the rear of the cabin. They were both double sets of contra-rotating curved blades in the usual style. The engines had a dual power source – the solar panels that covered most of the shell of the balloon of gas, along with back-up power provided by alcohol engines. A painted flash on the side of the cabin announced, in a nod to tradition, that the airship was operated by the 'Isle of Man Steam Packet Co-op'. In fact it was run by a mixture of people from the Republic and Atopia, with the Republic providing most of the material and equipment to operate the machines – it being in their interest to provide decent communications between the island and Atopia.

An oldish woman in yellow overalls stood at the flight steps. She smiled at me and gestured towards the long cabin above her. "You can sit anywhere you like. We're not going to be full today."

"Thanks."

"Flown before?" she asked.

"Once, a long time back."

She laughed. "An old hand, eh?"

"Too old."

She laughed again, showing a set of good teeth.

*   *   *

I sat by a window so I could get a good view. I hoped that it wouldn't be too bumpy a ride. That was a disadvantage of going by airship, they fly pretty low and get pushed about a little by the air currents. Still, you can't have everything. The use of airships, both piloted and remotely-controlled, has solved the problem of the continued need for some level of air transport, especially on short-haul routes. As speed is no longer a primary consideration, the airships are ideal, especially given their high levels of safety and eco-friendliness. High altitude remotely-controlled airships are also used to maintain satellite communications, providing a much cheaper and far more ecological solution to communication needs than old-style satellites that had to be taken into space by rocket or shuttle.

The cabin was beginning to fill up, and an old man dressed in brown and red velvet clothes came and sat next to me. He smelt of oranges and tobacco, which was fine by me.

"Hello, I'm Robin Goodfellow."

"Anne Riorden."

"Pleased to meet you. First time flying?"

"No, no. I've been up before."

"Do you like it?"

"It's okay, but I prefer my own two feet or a train for travelling."

"I know what you mean. Me, I've been taking a long journey round the whole of Europe, been wandering for three years now, nearly finished. Sort of pilgrimage, you could say, before I settle down again in Atopia. Before I go back to the woods." He smiled, but more to himself than me. I hoped that I wasn't going to get a blow-by-blow account of his travels, but fortunately he fell asleep just after the airship took off, and I was able to gaze happily out of the window.

*   *   *

We were soon heading out over Liverpool bay. We flew over a few ships waiting to pass through the estuary barrage that provides part of the city's energy needs. It had been raining, but the sun broke through the clouds above us and turned the dark waters of the bay into shimmering blue glass in which the tall, vertical sails of the ships were reflected, making them look like strange winged insects, white wings on red bodies. The ships make use of some very old technology from the twentieth century, with computers operating the stiff sails or engaging the auxiliary engines, as necessary. There aren't as many ships as there once were in Liverpool's first age of sail, but most long-distance travel is made by sea.

The ships moved into line and began to pass through the energy barrage, while the airship climbed higher. I read somewhere that an average city in Atopia gets its main energy from something like nine different sources, although of course heating requirements come from even more. A place like Liverpool gets most of its power from its estuary barrage, Liverpudlians' crap, the biomass plantations that fringe the city, and the wind farms that run along the coastline from the city to Southport. As usual, variety is the spice of life.

The airship arrived right on time at Ronaldsway Air Terminal, and I took the electric bus down the road to Castletown. According to the newspaper report, the capitalist had been sighted further up the east coast of the island in Douglas, but whether he was still there now was another question. I hoped that he was still on the island, as it was a small place and even such a greenhorn detective as myself should be able to find the man. Or then again, perhaps not. There was one good piece of news, however. I'd phoned Emilia from the Eastern Fed before I left Liverpool, and it looked as if the Angries were quietening down again. One of the big problems seemed to be that they couldn't find any weapons anywhere, which isn't

surprising since no one makes the things and most of the old stuff was melted down a long time ago. Anyway, the lack of guns seemed to have knocked the heart out of them, or perhaps they'd given themselves a fright, and wanted to go back to their usual life of navel-gazing. At any rate, the alarm over the Angries had subsided. But the Fed still wanted me to find the capitalist, to clear the whole thing up, and to make sure that it was all a one-off occurrence.

*   *   *

Once in Castletown I figured my best bet was to speak to the local press. The story about Alfred Mond preaching his capitalist gospel on the Douglas sea-front must have been filed by someone from the island.

Down by the harbour I found the printing works and offices of 'Republican Education', with its official coat of arms and the bilingual notices in Manx and English. It was strange seeing such an official title, such a statist title, in the utopian age, but then it was generally rumoured that the Manx were a conservative lot.

The office was big, but full of a variety of people all talking at once. After a while I managed to attract some attention, mainly by leering at a boy of about eighteen, who eventually stopped arguing about the layout for a pamphlet on cybernetics and came over to see what I wanted. His companion had obviously had enough, and announced that she was off to plant her early peas.

I was in luck, perhaps in more ways than one, except that I try to leave very young men alone. Anyway, Judas Iscariot (the kid had a sense of humour as well as a sense of history) listened to my story and said that he had heard about the chap calling himself Alfred Mond, in fact he'd thought of doing a story on him, but he'd had to do some work on one of the fishing boats so he hadn't had time. My appearance made him think that there really might be a good story to be had, so he got his coat and said that he'd come with me to Douglas. He had plenty of friends there and swore that if the capitalist was still on the island we'd find him. I was pleased, the whole thing looked as if it might be coming to an end.

We took the train to Douglas, and I thought I'd take the opportunity to chat up Judas – I'd decided that my success as a detective deserved a reward – but I didn't get too far on that score. Firstly he spotted my intentions straight off (I can't be that obvious, surely), and told me that his interests didn't extend to women. Then he decided that he better explain the Republic's set-up to an outsider like me. Utopian changes on the island had taken longer to come about than in Atopia. And, given the small size of the population and the sense of separateness that characterised the islanders' outlook, it had been decided that their utopia would be differently organised than it generally was elsewhere. So the Manx parliament was extended in numbers, the principle of people's delegates rather than parliamentary representatives was accepted, elections took place every year, and the parliament could be dissolved by a vote of the people organised by themselves at any time. No delegate could serve in the parliament for more than three years in succession, and for no more than nine years in total. The President of the Republic was elected every six months by the people and acted as a people's tribune. Every delegate, along with the president, had to take part in other, productive, activities and the delegates were forbidden to organise themselves into groups or parties.

Judas finished his brief description of the republican constitution just as the train pulled into Douglas station. I was getting pretty hungry, not to mention thirsty, so it was a relief when Judas said that it was best if we headed straight for The Orry where we'd find someone who'd know about my capitalist.

The Orry turned out to be a small dark pub within spitting distance of the sea, which groaned and crashed at the end of the narrow side street. The public bar was decorated with photographs and paintings of the small ships that they built at the Douglas Shipwrights Co-op. Wide-angled photographs of the co-op members of previous years hung over the bar itself. Most of the town's population appeared to be in the photographs.

There were only three women in the bar sitting around a driftwood table. Judas took me over to them and introduced me, then he left me to ask about the capitalist while he went behind the bar to fix some sandwiches and get a couple of beers. Eating the lamb and radish sandwiches and sipping at the glass of Manxman's Best, I listened while the three women argued about when and where the capitalist had been giving his little speeches about 'free enterprise', 'the profit motive' and the 'invisible hand', although two of the women maintained that he'd been on about the 'invisible foot'. At any rate, the general opinion was that he had a few screws loose, and that he was a harmless bloke who'd obviously gone overboard reading too much pre-utopian history. I winced at that and decided that I wouldn't mention my own interests in the pre-utopian set-up. The beer was good and I was enjoying listening to the women arguing about the details of the capitalist's stay in Douglas, but on the crucial point of where he was now they didn't have a clue. However, they reckoned that the President would be able to help out as he tended to be told about anything of importance that was going on, and plenty that wasn't important. Judas said that he'd take me to see the man himself, but we decided that it could wait a little while we all had another glass of the best.

*   *   *

"Pyotr!"

"Judas! How are you doing? It's ages since I've seen you, come here, let me look at you!"

The President left the huge pot that he'd been stirring on the co-op's cookers and drew Judas over to him. They kissed, and I pretended that I wasn't really there. After a while Judas remembered me and introduced me to Pyotr.

"Mr President, allow me to introduce you to Anne Riorden. Anne, meet the President."

We shook hands and laughed.

Judas turned back to Pyotr. "Anne's been sent by the Eastern Fed about that capitalist chap, Krupp or whatever he's calling himself. Apparently he's been wandering around Atopia trying to get people to act in a capitalist fashion."

"So what's the problem?" Pyotr asked, "No one's going to take any notice of him. No one did here in Douglas, hardly anyone understood what he was talking about."

"Well, he's not the only problem, the Angries are using him as an excuse to threaten all sorts of revolution against Atopia, although they may be going back to their normal self-imposed ghettos."

Pyotr turned the gas jet down under the pot, gave the contents a stir and looked at me carefully. "So you want to find this guy?"

"That's the idea."

"And what are you going to do when you find him? Arrest him?" he laughed.

"No of course not. All we want to find out is what is he really up to, why is he spouting on about capitalism, and whether he knows what effect he's been having?"

"Sounds pretty statist to me, if you want my opinion" Pyotr said.

I suddenly felt pretty uncomfortable. I'd been worrying about the ethics of what I was doing for a while, and the President had put his finger right on my dilemma.

"Yes, I agree, it doesn't look too healthy, perhaps. But I only want to talk to the man. That's all, nothing more."

Pyotr still looked doubtful.

Judas put his hand on Pyotr's arm. "Look, I think Anne's on the level here, she seems okay to me. If she says she just wants to talk to him I'm sure that's all she wants. Anyway, what else could she do?"

Pyotr chewed this one over, then spoke. "I trust your judgement, Judas, you know that, and you seem fine to me, Anne."

"Thanks," I replied, without any sense of irony.

"But you're too late to ask Krupp any questions, he's gone to Manchester, left this morning, flew straight there as far as I know."

"Damn! How do you know all this?"

"Well, I gave him breakfast here, seemed like an interesting guy, if a little weird, you know, with his totally out of date ideas, not to mention his clothes. They were really weird, he wasn't wearing long boots or skirts of anything, just a suit of grey cloth, but of a really old style."

"It's late twentieth century, as far as I can make out."

"Yes? Well it looks weird."

"So why was he going to Manchester, did he say?"

"Yes, I gave him an address he could go to, a friend of mine there. As I said, I reckoned that he was okay. Who isn't these days? Whatever he's saying, he still grew up in utopia."

"Can you give me that address?"

"No problem. Hang on, I'll get some paper."

Pyotr disappeared into the little office attached to the kitchen. Judas smiled at me, a nice smile. It was a pity that I wasn't going to be able to sleep with him, but then I had another journey ahead of me."

Pyotr came out of the office with the name and address on a piece of paper along with a few lines underneath saying that he had given me the address. It was a free school.

"Ask for Christine, she'll give you a warm welcome. When are you going?"

"As soon as possible."

He looked at his watch. "If you're quick you'll get the last flight today from Douglas Airport."

"Right."

We shook hands, Pyotr and Judas kissed and I said thanks. Judas took me down to the airport and I caught the day's last flight to Manchester. As we took off it began to rain heavily.

8.
Free School Stake-Out

The airship was quickly enveloped in thick cloud. The flight was almost empty so I stretched out across three seats and tried to get some sleep, but despite the glasses of Manxman's Best I just couldn't relax enough to fall asleep. I was now so close to the capitalist, only hours behind him, that I couldn't possibly fail to catch up with him now. Or so I hoped. For the first time since I'd started out from Oxford, I had a specific place where I should be able to find him – Krupp, or whoever. I searched in my pockets for the scrap of paper that Pyotr had given me, found it and sat staring at the address: Willow Brae Free School, Withington, Manchester. Free schools, the culmination of centuries of trying to work out just what education is. It seems so simple now, but conditions have changed, so free schools can flourish.

Free schools have a very long history. You could argue that they are merely the inheritors of pre-industrial methods of secular education when children simply learned as they grew to take their place in the adult world. That style of education was, of course, suited to the limited needs of society, just as education for clerics was designed for the ruling hierarchies of church and state. In that sense, it's true that society gets the education it needs, for the education systems of industrial and parliamentary society reflected class divisions, and the military, religious and economic concerns of the ruling classes in those societies. And today, of course, utopian society is reflected in and reinforced by a utopian approach to learning.

None of the ideas and ideals underpinning free schools are new, but it is only since the development and establishment of Atopia that those principles have been successfully applied – there being no mismatch between free education and the society that the products of that education have to live in. The basic principle is, as in the rest of utopia, free choice based on each individual having the security of life to make such a choice. Free choice means choosing when, and if, one wants to go to the free school. You might choose to spend time

there for comparatively long periods – weeks or even months. Or perhaps just a few hours a week, or, then again, not at all. And you may choose to use the facilities at the age of ten or twenty or sixty. There are no syllabuses, no curriculums, you choose what suits your requirements and your desires. Or perhaps someone has started to turn up at school who has great knowledge about the medieval world or geology or whatever, and you wish to take advantage of conversations with that person. Knowledge that is freely given and received.

In one sense the whole of the social life of Atopia is an educative process, a constant leading out of its people. If you wish to develop new skills then you can find help and training in that skill wherever it is practised. My own case is typical. In my early teens I'd spent much time with the railways and had learnt a variety of skills, the same goes for my computer knowledge, while my passion for history was satisfied by the men and women who gathered around the great libraries in Oxford whose openness and willingness to share their knowledge with anyone was typical of free schools everywhere.

*   *   *

It was getting dark when we arrived at Ringway Airport, but I didn't want the capitalist to evade me again so I took a bus straight to Withington. With any luck I would be able to sleep overnight at the free school, even if I couldn't find my capitalist immediately.

The bus glided away from Ringway, running almost silently on its electric batteries. Like all transport it was multi-energy sourced, charging its batteries from the city's electricity which was, in turn, provided by a multitude of environmentally positive sources. In addition the bus was roofed with solar panels that also charged the batteries. There were few bikes on the road, so apart from other public vehicles it was quite clear, and we ran along steadily at about thirty miles an hour. Manchester was famed for having taken the urban forest arguments further than any other city in Atopia, and the bus ran through countless acres of trees and urban woodland. Biomass plantations occurred frequently, farmed in blocks that were planted between small housing schemes. The houses themselves were usually wooden built, with occasional remnants of pre-utopian housing still standing, upgraded and often used for community purposes. All the

streets were lined with trees, mainly fruit trees that were laced pink
and white with spring blossom, while gardens were usually bordered
with bushes or evergreen hedges.

Driving through these streets and squares, it was difficult to imagine
that in the past Manchester had been home to some of the worst
urban problems in the country. But out of those problems had come
key realisations that had put us all on the road to Atopia. The great
drugs wars had, at first, led to widespread calls for more and more
police repression. The special paramilitary Armed Drugs Unit was
something that was specifically created to deal with the drugs fighting
in Manchester and London. But ADU violence simply led to even
more violence, and the final collapse of public order in the city. The
government had wanted to impose martial law in Manchester but the
army, desperately trying to find volunteers to fight with the Russian
Federation on its Chinese and Asian borders, had refused to be drawn
into what it saw as an unsolvable problem. Indeed Field Marshal
Singh had spoken out publicly against the existence of drug laws.
His comments, plus the obvious fact that the government could no
longer police its major cities, led finally to the abandonment of the
drug laws. It didn't stop the fighting immediately, however, for the
drugs gangs continued to kill one another. Their continued belligerence
was their undoing, in fact, as they fought each other to a standstill,
emerging too weak to find any substitute for the illegal drugs market,
which had now disappeared. It then became clear that the people of
Manchester had been taking significant steps to protect and develop
their communities from both the criminals and the authorities. They
had almost withdrawn from a money and profit based economy, and
were beginning the regeneration of their communities on the basis
of self-help, co-operation and pride. A seachange had taken place in
the cultural and economic life of the city, in keeping with the new
methods of living that were gradually emerging throughout the
country as government collapsed under its own weight and people
sought to replace chaos with anarchic forms of living.

That was all history, and chaos was long gone, gone forever I hoped.
But Atopia wasn't a stagnant society, new developments, new changes
were taking place all the time, that was one of our society's greatest
strengths. But, sitting in the bus watching the dark trees pass, I

wondered if it might be a weakness as well. What if the capitalist did start to make converts, convince people that things could be done in a capitalist way, like in pre-utopian days? Was it possible that people could begin to turn their backs on Atopia, just as they had turned away from the old forms of living? Perhaps it was. I shivered. I was tired and hungry, but I had to talk to this capitalist, this loose cannon.

The driver of the bus called back, telling me that he'd let me off at the edge of Withington Park, which was just ahead. I pulled my bag down and struggled to the door. The bus drew into the kerb and the driver leaned over to me.

"See that path through the trees?"

"By the lights?"

"Yes, just follow it to the other side of the park. When you come out on that side you'll see The Black Bear pub opposite. Cross over and go down that road, the school's at the bottom, you can't miss is, it's a big old building surrounded by cherry trees."

"Thanks."

"That's okay. Be seeing you, chuck."

The bus drew silently away, and I began to follow the path through the dark trees. I wondered what The Black Bear was like, but the thought that the capitalist might only be a few hundred yards away kept me going past the pub, and down the road to the school.

The bus driver had been right, I couldn't miss the school. The old brick-built building was almost hidden by dozens of broad sweeping cherry trees that were already covered by thick pink and white blossom. Like all cities in Atopia, there wasn't much need for many street lights, so the strange luminescence of the cherry blossom seemed to light up the area. I looked at my watch, eight-thirty, there would be plenty of people still in the school.

I walked up the main steps, and was met by a mass of people who came pouring out laughing and talking, some of them about Piers Plowman. The crowd thinned and I got into the building. I took the letter from Pyotr out of my pocket, and stared at the information board hanging in the foyer. The board had been hand painted by someone who thought that paintings of trailing flowers, in a William Morris style, intertwining with the letters of the board was a good idea. It was a beautiful piece of work, but it certainly made the sign difficult to read. Eventually, however, I worked out that the bookings office was on the first floor.

I pushed open the office door and was met with a broad smile from a broad woman with blonde hair. She looked at me as if I was a favourite child, or perhaps she was just contented like the rest of us.

"Hi, can I help?"

"Yes. My name's Anne Riorden. I'm looking for someone called Christine."

"You've found me."

"Oh right, good. Pyotr said I should look you up, that you might be able to help me." I handed her the little letter from Pyotr.

Christine beamed even more and stood up, wagging the letter at me and simultaneously ushering me into a deep winged chair.

"Have you just come from the Republic? Oh, you must be tired. Here I'll get you a cup of tea. Is that okay?"

I said it was, and she bustled around a hot plate making tea and reading the letter at the same time.

We drank tea and ate some biscuits, while Christine grilled me about Pyotr. She was amused that he had become President and kept saying 'Pyotr, oh I mean Mr President'. She talked and she laughed and smiled, and under the ceaseless assault I began to feel myself relaxing, beginning to feel sleepy. But then I remembered what I was there for, and steeled myself to tell Christine about the capitalist. Eventually I managed to turn the conversation away from Pyotr and around to the capitalist. I described him, and explained why the Eastern Fed were interested in finding out what he was up to. Christine stopped talking for a while, mulling the news over.

"Well that sounds odd. It certainly sounds like the same chap that I met, Dick Branson he was calling himself, but he seemed like such a nice man. I'm sure he doesn't mean any harm. He can't do." Christine shook her head vigorously.

"You might be right, Christine, but I've got to check it out, make sure that he's okay, ask him why he's going around talking capitalism up."

She still didn't seem happy. I didn't feel that happy myself, the whole thing smacked of the past and I wasn't sure that I really liked being a detective, not even a private one, it didn't seem right. I didn't know what else I could say to convince Christine, so I just smiled at her and tried to look innocent and unthreatening.

"Well," she said, "you've come an awful long way, and I can't see the harm in talking to him."

"Good, thanks."

She stood up, brushing biscuit crumbs onto the floor. "I don't think he's here at the moment. He left his bags in the common room, as I said that he could sleep here tonight, there's good, long sofas and blankets and things. So he'll be back sometime, perhaps you'd like to wait for him there. She smiled again. "You look as if you're tired too, you could bunk down there until he comes in, and I'll fix you some sandwiches."

"That's great. You're right, I could do with a sleep."

Christine took me to the common room, a big room full of bookcases, sofas and deep chairs. I settled in one of the chairs, and Christine went to get me something to eat. She came back with stilton cheese, onion and bread, and a bottle of Prisoners' Escape, brewed at the Strangeways Brewery it said on the bottle. I thanked her and she said that she had a few things to do in the office before she went home.

I ate the bread and cheese, and drank the bottle of beer. A few people wandered in and out of the common room carrying books, swapping books with those on the shelves and wishing me 'goodnight'. The beer and the food felt good inside me, and I fetched a blanket and put it over me while I waited. Listening to the echoes of voices in the big building, I slowly drifted off to sleep.

*   *   *

I was suddenly awake in the dark, not knowing for a moment where I was. I shifted in the chair, pushing the rough blanket away from my face. I remembered the free school, Christine and the beer, wondering what had woken me so suddenly. Then I heard a noise outside the door which loomed as a dark rectangle in the wall of books opposite me. I tried to focus my eyes in the dark, but couldn't make out the door handle, although I knew it was slowly turning.

The door opened, swinging back silently. A tall, dark figure filled the open doorway. The figure was wearing an old-style hat, and had one hand on the door handle, the other in his pocket. He took a few steps into the room and closed the door behind him.

9.
'Hi There, Little Sister'

I waited in the darkness. I was glad that I wasn't really a twentieth century peeper, because he would have made his entry with a gun. But, still, I was uneasy and unsure what to do next. Then the lights flicked on, and I saw the capitalist for the first time. He was tall and slim and dressed in a grey old-style suit. I couldn't see his face clearly as it was obscured by the brim of his hat, but his mouth looked pleasant enough. He smiled, took a few steps forward and said "Hi there, little sister. I hear you've been looking for me."

That threw me, both his reference to Raymond Chandler's novel, and the soft smile and voice. But I pulled myself back together, stood up and stepped towards him, my mind groping unsuccessfully for some detective-style repartee.

"Natch, we've just been travelling the same road. It's all a big coincidence." I said, leering in what I imagined was a hard-boiled detective pose.

He laughed and took off his hat. His skin was very pale, Scottish almost, and he had light coloured hair combed carefully back from his forehead. It was difficult to tell what colour his eyes were, some shade between blue and grey. But despite the washed-out appearance of his clothes and face, there was something attractive about him. Perhaps that made him dangerous, I wouldn't know, not having met anyone dangerous before in Atopia.

"Hey, I'm cold, do you fancy a coffee?" he said, walking over to the kettle and cups on the long table.

"Sure, why not."

I followed him over to the table and stood near him while he made the coffee.

"What are you calling yourself at the moment, Frick, Nuffield, Carnegie or what?"

He laughed again, a low, running laugh. "Whatever. What do you think suits me best?"

I looked at his smooth, pale face with the smiling mouth. "To be honest, none of them. From what I know of the capitalist era, I'd say that you've got the wrong sort of face altogether, not hard-faced enough by far. You're no Carnegie or Frick, or any of the others from the capitalists' golden age. Give you a change of clothes and you could be any utopian."

"Perhaps I am," he answered, passing me a coffee.

"Shall we take a seat?"

I followed him over to the deep chairs and took one facing him. Now I had found the capitalist, or rather now he'd found me, I wasn't sure what to do with him, what to ask him, so I plumped for the obvious.

"Why?"

"Why the capitalism?"

"Yeah, why the capitalism." We certainly had some crackling dialogue going, Bill Pronzini would have been proud of me.

"Well let me ask you one" he said. "Why the private eye? Why the mid-twentieth century California Sunset Strip trip?"

I was in check and I was hoping that it wasn't going to be check-mate. I decided to level with him, because that was the utopian way and because I realised that I couldn't take my eyes off that smiling mouth.

"If anyone normally asks that question I give them the spiel about being interested in history, you know, that's my thing, that's what I teach when I get the chance."

"But *I'm* asking."

"Just for you then." I smiled back at him.

"Just for you, the fact is that I like it, I get off on it. Damn it, sometimes I imagine that I'd really like to drive a convertible down to the Bay."

"So it's more than history for you, more than looking into the pre-utopian past?"

I had to think that one over. I didn't like the implications for me. I decided to ask him a question instead.

"I've answered one of your questions, but I'm supposed to be asking them. So do us both a favour and answer mine. Why the capitalism, and do you know the trouble you've been causing?"

He smiled again, and I wished that he'd stop it, it was affecting my body temperature.

"That's two questions, sister."

"What the hell! Answer them."

"Perhaps I should, though you've no right to any explanations."

I didn't like that, and I told him, "I mightn't have any warrant like in the old days, but I've followed you half way around Atopia. If anyone's got any rights in this, it's me."

He laughed, showing nice teeth.

"I'll answer your second question first. And the answer is that I haven't caused any trouble, not permanent anyway."

"You've not heard about the Angries and their little revolution then?" I countered. But he was better informed that I thought.

He waved his hand in front of his face, swatting imaginary mosquitoes. "What revolution? You know as well as I do that they were just having their annual outing, they're no more going to launch a revolution now than they were in pre-utopian days. It's all posturing, all hot air. Okay I gave them an excuse, but they'd have found another if I hadn't been around."

"It was a bit more than that this time. At least the Eastern Fed thought so. Enough to send me after you," I said, rather lamely.

He snorted in derision. "Angries!"

"Okay, we'll let that go as you're right, they've gone back to normal. But why the capitalism?"

He looked at me closely as if he were trying to decide just what sort of woman I was. Then he gazed into his coffee cup. I said nothing, it was obvious that he was trying to compose a decent answer. Eventually he looked up again, his face smooth and serious.

"I'm not sure myself, and I'm not sure that I can provide a convincing answer." He shrugged his shoulders. "It all sounds so unreal in the reality of Atopia. Capitalism." He mouthed the word again, silently, as if it was some long- forgotten magic incantation that he'd discovered. It was certainly long-forgotten, and perhaps it was a form of black magic.

"I suppose it was a combination of nostalgia for the past, a past that I never knew, and the effect of ideology." He smiled again. "Sorry about using all these dirty words, but that's about it, a sort of historical glamour mixed with the effects of ideology. You see, I'd started to read up about the ideological underpinnings of capitalism, how they justified all the absurd things that utopia did away with, how they saw people's motivations, what the aims of that system was, those sort of things. I really got into it, started to do nothing else but read up on it, watch old video material on capitalism. I got really hooked, couldn't get enough of the stuff."

I butted in. "There's nothing unusual about that. I've been like that myself. We all go through that sort of phase, it's one of the ways we learn."

He shook his head. "No, it was more than that, or it became more than that. I began to realise that I was looking at utopia in a different light, I began to think about costs, product, marginal returns," he paused, "profits even. Profits! See, you can see how bad I got."

"You're speaking in the past tense" I said.

But he wasn't going to be interrupted in his confession. "Yes, I'll get on to that in a minute. But, like I said, I'd got the ideology bug really bad, I just had to go out and tell everyone how they were making a mess of things, how things could be much more fulfilling if we forgot about our little small-scale communal way of doing things, and thought big, thought profit and loss, thought success, thought entrepreneurship, all that sort of stuff."

He seemed to be talking to himself as much as me, talking himself through his ordeal, reliving his period of insanity.

"Then I got to thinking how Atopia had come about, how the old system had begun to crumble, and people had simply gone off to make new relationships, new ways of doing things, behaving differently – just like Gustav Landauer said. So I thought that I'd be able to get out there and convince people to behave differently, except this time I'd get them to behave in a capitalist way, get them to think about the main chance, about profits and rackets, that way of thinking. But I must have been out of my mind. In Atopia! Me, trying to get people to act capitalist – not a hope." He grinned. "I guess I must be the last capitalist, or rather I *was* the last capitalist."

I smiled at him. "There's that past tense again."

"Yes. The past tense. We'll never see capitalism again, or ideologues, and now I'm fine again, now I've realised what a bloody fool I've been, I guess Atopia has seen the last of the last capitalist."

He took off his old-style tie and rolled it into a ball.

"Damn, I need to get out of this silly suit. No wonder the capitalists were such a bunch of bastards, wearing one of these things all your life would turn anyone nuts."

We both laughed.

"Perhaps I could help you with that."

"With what?"

"Helping you out of your suit. And maybe something more. It sounds as if you need some sex and beer therapy after your ordeal."

He grinned at me, his mouth wide and smiling. "And where could I get that?"

"Oh I know a little place, a barge on a river. It's called Berkman's Barge and I'm the therapist."

"Sounds fine to me" he said, stepping out of his trousers.

"Welcome back to Atopia!"

Steve Cullen has also written

CHILDREN IN SOCIETY: A LIBERTARIAN CRITIQUE

"In our society children are largely a silent group, whose needs and wants are entirely determined by adults. At every stage adults seek to mould children to the priorities of an alien, adult world. The baby must be trained to a 'routine', the child must be 'disciplined', a place must be found at nursery or creche as soon as possible, it must be fed into eleven or more years of compulsory education. Protestations from the child are met with the over-riding power of the adult, based ultimately, and usually, on physical coercion. But there is also a justification, for not all adults are happy with the formula 'Because I tell you to', instead the child can be informed in his or her misery that 'It's for your own good'.

Such an approach arises from a refusal to treat children as having equal status and rights as any adult. The essential difference between an adult and a child is one of time and experience, but beyond that there is no difference. Few adults would accept that a more experienced adult, for instance in educational terms, should be treated with substantially more respect than a less experienced adult, yet that view is the norm as far as children are concerned."

48 pages   **ISBN 0 900384 62 X**   **£1.20**

FREEDOM PRESS
84b Whitechapel High Street, London E1 7QX

VISIONS OF POESY
AN ANTHOLOGY OF TWENTIETH CENTURY ANARCHIST POETRY

EDITED BY
CLIFFORD HARPER, DENNIS GOULD and JEFF CLOVES

Seven years in preparation, this eagerly awaited collection is published at a time when popular interest in poetry is at an all time high. The publishers, Freedom Press, believe that *Visions of Poesy* will prove to be a book very much for our times. The editors have chosen over 200 poems from seventy of the best loved poets of this century, all of them committed to an anarchist vision of society. While the poetry in this book spans our entire century, it echoes very strongly the current wave of new poetry. It includes examples of the agitational verse of the Industrial Workers of the World from around 1910, remarkable for its wit and invention, a typical long poem from avant-garde composer John Cage, poems from the '30s and '40s by such poets as Alex Comfort and Herbert Read, the lyrical work of Kenneth Patchen, a wide choice from the Beat poets, including Lawrence Ferlinghetti, Allen Ginsberg and Gary Snyder, a representative selection of post-war English poets, among them Adrian Henri, Bernard Kops, Christopher Logue, Adrian Mitchell, Allan Sillitoe, Stevie Smith and Muriel Spark. The book also contains voices from many of the political causes of recent times, the Vietnam War and the upsurges of the '60s, the feminist wave of the '70s, the anti-nuclear movement and punk. Overall *Visions of Poesy* is informed by an anarchist perspective: all of the poets are or were anarchists. This does not mean that the poetry is simply political and crudely didactic, rather it displays a rejection of the current order combined with a searching for something better.

All of the poetry is in the English language, the book contains no translated work. While the majority of the poets are either English or American, there are many poets from other countries, including Canada, Ireland, Wales, Scotland and New Zealand.

The editors of *Visions of Poesy* have themselves all been deeply involved in both poetry and anarchism for many years. Dennis Gould and Jeff Cloves have been writing and publishing poetry since the mid '60s and have been reading their poetry to appreciative audiences throughout that time. Clifford Harper, an artist and anarchist, has been collecting anarchist poetry for over 25 years.

Freedom Press   **ISBN 0 900384 75 1**   **317 pages**   **£8.00**

The Blue Cow
by John Olday

This unusual Freedom Press title is a work of genius. Produced fifty years ago, it remained forgotten in a filing cabinet until recently found by mistake. Although intended for the young, it is, in fact, both by the brilliance of the drawings and the surrealism of the text, surely even more fascinating to adults than to their offspring!

66 pages   **ISBN 0 900384 86 7**   **£3.50**

A Weekend Photographer's Notebook
170 photographs by Vernon Richards

The division between amateur and professional has always been a blurred one in photography and the amateurs, particularly in the nineteenth century, often initiated both aesthetic and technical advances. Vernon Richards is happy to see himself in this tradition. He makes no claim to break new ground but his humane eye allows important qualities to shine through his photographs. Their straightforward honesty and compassion vividly reveal the great interest in, and friendship towards, his fellow men and the world about us. This weekend 'button-presser' shows us how much can be achieved by an energetic enthusiast whose simple equipment would be considered laughable by today's gadget-laden photographers, both amateur and professional.

Freedom Press   112 A4 pages   ISBN 0 900384 87 5   £6.95

ABOUT FREEDOM PRESS

- FREEDOM PRESS are the publishers of the fortnightly journal *Freedom* and of the anarchist quarterly *The Raven*.

- FREEDOM PRESS are the publishers of books and pamphlets on anarchism and allied subjects. Our current list comprises some sixty titles.

- FREEDOM PRESS BOOKSHOP (open Monday to Saturday) carries a comprehensive stock of anarchist literature from this country, the USA and Canada. We also issue lists for the benefit of our mail order customers.

- FREEDOM PRESS DISTRIBUTORS are the European sales representatives for a number of small publishers in this country.

- This book has been printed by ALDGATE PRESS, a successful co-operative venture which also undertakes commercial printing work.

All particulars from
FREEDOM PRESS
84b Whitechapel High Street, London E1 7QX